Praise for
The Power of Potential

"Through demystifying the secrets of modeling, the book *The Power of Potential* will take you on a journey of discovery, revolutionising the way you learn. Prepare to be surprised as you begin to discover the ways that you can uncover 'the difference that makes the difference.' David has expertly provided you with an invitation to set your trajectory and write your own map; whilst offering you all the resources you will need to navigate, as you treasure hunt for the magic that denotes 'mastery' and bring your newfound awareness into the way you show up in the world. A joy to read, this book is for all those who embody curiosity, a desire to learn, and a passion to succeed."

—**Lizzi Larbalestier,** Blue Health Executive Coach™ and
Ocean Advocate, Founder at Going Coastal Blue

"Not just a must-read, but a book you will want to pull off your bookshelf and read again and again throughout your journey in life. David masterfully lays out a practical blueprint to acquire the critical thinking skills essential to achieve your full potential in both your professional and personal life. *The Power of Potential* is an absolute must for anyone seeking a positive and lasting impact on their path to success!"

—**Liv A. Watson,** Sr. Director of Strategic Customer Initiatives

"The path to mastering any target skill has seemingly lacked structure, felt non-linear and caused more than one professional on the road to personal growth to give up. But in today's world, we are required to take on more responsibility and learn new skills faster. Often, 'give up', live with the 'imposter syndrome' dread, or 'just try harder' aren't viable options. How do you become an expert when it really matters? In *The Power of Potential*, David lays out a logical learning model and series of concrete steps anyone can take towards acquiring any target skill—be it public speaking or making an omelet. He has done a masterful job fusing human psychology with practical tips & exercises to empower the reader to dissect and master any target skill they desire."

—**Derek Sidebottom,** Chief Human Resources Officer

"We are told to learn continuously that acquiring new skills will enhance both our career and increase our own personal happiness. However, learning new skills can be a daunting ask, causing many of us to cower in the moment and stick to what we know . . . what is comfortable. However, in that mindset we only hurt and limit ourselves. In *The Power of Potential*, David skillfully helps the reader confront their emotions and removes the mental obstacles of mastering new skills by breaking down every element to its core, offering us a tangible and personalized roadmap of learning. With the fear removed, individuals take leaps that generate ideas, skills and eventually new habits, thus meeting their true potential."

—**Jennifer Farris,** Co-Founder of FarsideHR

THE
POWER OF
POTENTIAL

A STRAIGHTFORWARD METHOD
FOR MASTERING SKILLS
FROM PERSONAL TO PROFESSIONAL

DAVID WRAY

RIVER GROVE
BOOKS

This publication is designed to provide accurate and authoritative information in regard to the subject matter covered. It is sold with the understanding that the publisher and author are not engaged in rendering legal, accounting, or other professional services. Nothing herein shall create an attorney-client relationship, and nothing herein shall constitute legal advice or a solicitation to offer legal advice. If legal advice or other expert assistance is required, the services of a competent professional should be sought.

Published by River Grove Books
Austin, TX
www.rivergrovebooks.com

Distributed by River Grove Books

Design and composition by Greenleaf Book Group and Kim Lance
Cover design by Greenleaf Book Group and Kim Lance
Cover illustration by iStock / Getty Images Plus / Sylverarts

Publisher's Cataloging-in-Publication data is available.

Print ISBN: 978-1-63299-361-8

eBook ISBN: 978-1-63299-362-5

First Edition

To Martha, my wife and best friend, your encouragement and support gave me the time to "give it a go," I love you.

To anyone who picks up this book, here's hoping you take hold of the model, make it your own, and give it a try. You have everything to gain.

Enjoy!
David

"Here's to the crazy ones.
The misfits. The rebels.
The troublemakers. The round pegs
in the square holes. The ones who
see things differently . . . Because
the people who are crazy enough to
think they can change the world,
are the ones who do."

—Apple Inc.

Contents

Preface

I wrote this book to solve a seemingly simple problem: How could I learn to perfect my skills faster and more easily? Skills acquisition is time-consuming, expensive, and often winds up being abandoned far too fast. Like most people, I've had my fair share of starting to learn something, only to give up in frustration over the enormous effort and infuriating complexity involved in mastering it. The solution eventually came to me through applying Neuro-linguistic Programming tips, techniques, and tools, coupled with practical experience. As a result, I've significantly improved my own ability not only to quickly learn new skills but also to polish up existing ones. Instances of the uses I've made of the model so far: perfecting the art of public speaking, making healthy lifestyle changes, learning another language, perfecting buoyancy as a diver, completing a book, and developing a business (and helping others to do the same).

Basically, the system works stunningly well—once you understand its secrets.

While I can't promise you fame and fortune, I *can* promise you the tools to help you do as I have done. I invite you to learn how to acquire and master those skills that you want, faster and more easily than you ever imagined. And who doesn't want to learn and master a skill, to finish something new and creative, to further a career, to make more money, or simply to excel at something you love? The good news: The tools you need to do just that lie here within these pages.

Regret will be a thing of the past. This really is the last "how-to" book you'll ever need! What you choose to do with your new skills, of course, is up to you.

Each chapter provides vital secrets that will empower you to get a jump-start on the competition and to control your future. In fact, if you utilize the formulas revealed here, it's highly likely you'll find yourself enjoying the rest of your life, unburdened with what-if regrets and relishing incredible experiences. So, let's get started!

Introduction

You've undoubtedly seen a talented individual in action and secretly wished that you could achieve as easily and effortlessly as they seem to. Well, you can! You can replicate any skill. You simply need to understand both the visible and invisible workings that an expert utilizes when doing their thing.

This book will help you identify the invisible processing through which an individual's worldview influences that person's actions. By understanding this (and you will when you've read this book), we can get straight to the heart of unlocking your ability to master the skills you really want.

You will learn about the real, but invisible, internal processing we all go through when receiving information (an "external event"). These externalities occur daily and range from benign (something as simple as being cut off in traffic) to life changing (such as hearing a terminal medical diagnosis). We each react differently to the same event. Why? The difference is in how we process things in light of our view of the world. We each filter information as we process it; for example, some individuals may choose to ignore information or may generalize by associating it to a past experience. Each filter is influenced by how we see ourselves, what we believe, what we value, powerful memories (positive or negative), and how we speak to ourselves (for example, is our inner chatter self-critical or self-respecting). As if all this rapid processing weren't enough, our current state of mind also affects outcome. If we are cut off in traffic on a day when we've just heard great news, the other driver's lack of consideration will probably roll off like water from a duck's back. If we've just received news of a layoff, that relatively minor traffic slight could become a trigger to an uncharacteristically angry outburst. These rapid information-processing systems result in the behaviors we exhibit and in turn how others perceive us.

Our journey together will empower you with the knowledge and tools needed to harness these inner systems to your advantage.

The Journey

In Part One, you'll learn how to create a model to replicate any skill by

- Generating ideas
- Clarifying your chosen idea
- Developing a model of the skill/idea
- Testing/ensuring that your model works

In Part Two, you'll learn how to take your big idea and embed the skills yourself by

- Leveraging your motivational and change styles, igniting a fire for self-change
- Establishing and executing a winning game plan
- Surrounding yourself with the best support system
- Enjoying success and helping others do the same

Having set the context, let's jump right in!

Part One

Understanding: How to Master Any Skill

Can you recognize and describe the visible and invisible "things" that go into performing a skill?

Let's consider a simple, random example: preparing and cooking a Spanish omelet. This process can be broken down into several actions with associated decisions (known as micro-moments):

- Ingredients: fresh, frozen, organic?
- Utensils: hand tools or blender?
- Preparation: whip, fold, or blend? Preferred order?
- Cooking: when to turn? How long to cook?
- Serving: presentation?

Those are the obvious external considerations. Ready to get started?

But wait, hold your horses! What about the thought processes, feelings, beliefs, values, and motivators underpinning an expert chef's actions? Which of these invisible attributes assists in their success in consistently achieving such a seemingly effortless level of culinary skill?

In Part One, we will cover the external and internal conditions that contribute to expert-level mastery of a given skill. You'll learn how to do the following:

1. Prepare yourself for the discovery process.

2. Find and speak to experts about their performance.

3. Organize your findings into a road map to mastery.

4. Create a model that you can replicate on your own path to expert status in that skill area.

Chapter 1

Identifying Which Skill to Model

Congratulations on the decision to master a skill you admire in others! This is the first step in one of the most crucial investments you could possibly make: the decision to invest in *you*.

Let's now address the elephant-in-the-room question: What's in it for you, and is it worth your time and energy to take this journey? Each day, millions of people ask this question when weighing everyday decisions. If accelerating your career progression, making more money, or simply excelling at something you love appeals to you, then you've chosen wisely.

Let's begin this transforming journey. It starts by understanding that being as specific as possible in the earliest stages about the precise skill you wish to develop (or "model") produces a much more meaningful outcome later on. (Of course, you might instead find it interesting to model a skill you already have with the intention of sharpening it further.)

BRAINSTORMING, PREPARING, AND NARROWING YOUR CHOSEN IDEA

Before we begin the dissection process of capturing specific "moments in time," let's consider a couple of examples that could suggest methods by which expertise might be captured.

- **Public Speaking:** Interestingly, this is the skill that evokes admiration, even jealousy, more than almost any other. Yet the presentation process itself is remarkably similar between presenters in most cases. So why is the interest in and overall quality of the speakers so varied?

- **Personal Health:** This must be a near-universal goal, yet for most people it remains a common source of both well-intentioned resolutions and frustrating missteps! From a modeling point of view, it would prove useful to analyze those elements and behaviors consistently found in the fittest individuals with the healthiest outcomes. (And yes, becoming healthy *can* be regarded as a life skill.)

The list of potential skills to model is limited only by your imagination. You may be wondering why one can't simply model the process consecutively, from A to Z, rather than by choosing a "moment in time." In fairness, this is perfectly possible, utilizing several interlocking models. The modular approach taken in this book simply recognizes the practical limitations of time, effort, and expense. The smoothest and fastest route to mastery most often lies in the "moment in time" method. This is why in interviews, we will ask our expert to concentrate on their performance in a moment of utter mastery.

In addition, a clearly defined scope allows you to select the "right" area of the expert's expertise needed to capture the best end-to-end model for the specific skill that you have determined to master.

THE BEGINNING

You can start the modeling process by brainstorming ideas on flip charts, paper, or mobile devices—the medium chosen is of no real importance. At this stage all ideas deserve to be captured; they can be refined (or deleted) later. The objective is to start thinking about which moment(s) you could, and then would, like to model for the outcomes that most appeal to you.

YOUR TURN, GIVE IT A TRY!
Take four minutes to jot down your ideas.
No need to organize them at this point, simply let
your creativity run wild and capture the skill ideas
that come to mind.

The six elements to consider during the "idea generation" stage are—

- Raw inputs
- Tools
- Preparation
- Processing
- Delivery
- Closing

Figures 1.1 and 1.2 show suggestions for how to brainstorm a skill and how to structure at a high level your options in preparation for selecting a specific "moment in time."

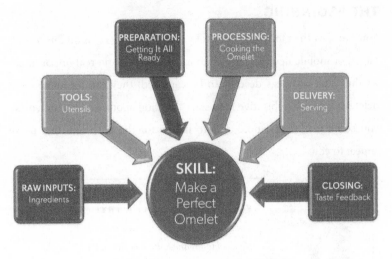

Figure 1.1. Process steps—perfect omelets.

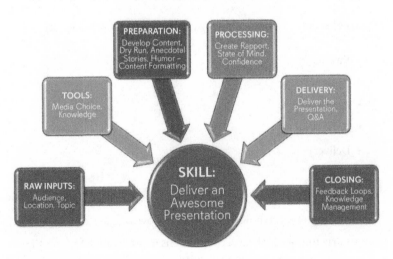

Figure 1.2. Process steps—awesome presentations.

YOUR TURN, GIVE IT A TRY!
Develop a simple process diagram for one of the skill development ideas you've brainstormed.

With at least a few of your ideas captured on paper, let's look at how to further scale down the process encapsulating the skill into a "moment in time."

NARROWING INTO A SPECIFIC MOMENT

Narrowing the idea from general to specific is one of the most critical steps in your journey. It frames the scope for your area of interest as well as influences your selected interviewees and your final model. The more precisely you develop the idea, the more value you'll typically glean from the process. An unfocused idea all too frequently generates a vague and nonspecific model, which is unlikely to dramatically improve your own skill(s), let alone enable you to pass on your fresh expertise to anyone else. Reining in a wide scope to a specific moment will produce a richer model and one potentially transferable to others.

To identify the external (or visible) and internal (or invisible) attributes within your chosen "moment," you need to develop a flow of inputs and outputs. Ask yourself the following questions:

- What activities go into making those few, crucial minutes within in the moment happen?
- What is the outcome from the activities within those few minutes?
- What other activities or events could potentially affect outcomes on the day that the skill moment is occurring?

Public speaking

Let's pick up this example again. In this skill, the steps are broken into micro-moments or steps, the aggregate of which results in excellence. Becoming a master presenter requires confident skills within each segment (or micro-step) of the process. Yet even among experts, there are differing levels of skills in different segments.

For example, John may be perfectly comfortable delivering the presentation content, yet feel far less assured with regard to the question-and-answer (Q&A) element. John comes to you asking for help to be the best he can be in Q&A management. He strongly feels a need to improve in both his ability and confidence. The modeling moment in time in this case becomes the ten minutes of live Q&A.

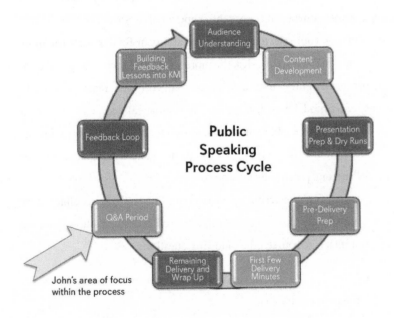

Figure 1.3. The public speaking cycle.

This can be broken down further into incremental micro-moments (before, during, and after the actual Q&A slot), each of which can be mastered and taught to others on a stand-alone basis or as part of a wider skill-development program. While working through this disaggregation, John ultimately recognizes that his real issue is his state of mind (his self-talk) immediately prior to the Q&As.

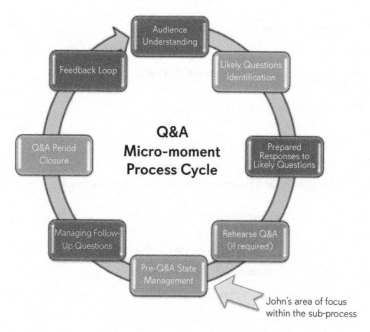

Figure 1.4. Question & answer micro-moments of public speaking.

Let's analyze a second example, using a slightly different goal.

Becoming healthier (fitter)

Most people understand the importance of such behaviors as eating a balanced diet, regular exercise, or not smoking. If we expand our earlier example to further outline ten micro-moments suitable for modeling in this area, they might look something like this:

With regard to goal-setting skills:

1. Developing positive health-oriented fitness objectives
2. Developing individual fitness goals using a SMART[1] approach

With regard to establishing a supportive environment:

3. Implementing personal support systems
4. Modifying routines to include new and healthier behaviors
5. Identifying feedback mechanisms to self-assess progress

With regard to motivational factors:

6. Evaluating payoffs associated with specific fitness-based behavioral changes
7. Identifying and incorporating personal motivations

With regard to tracking systems:

8. Developing and tracking against an action plan
9. Planning deviation management (if required)
10. Correcting action plan (if required)

Laying out the micro-moments in this format may stimulate further reflection on what may be missing in your world and needs focus. For example, motivation may be a weakness requiring skill improvement—fortunately, we look at motivators in Chapter 9.

These illustrations are designed to shed light on a couple of end-to-end

---

1   SMART = Specific, Measurable, Achievable, Realistic, and Time-bound. George T. Doran, 1981.

processes where specific modellable skills may be gained. The two different formats provide you with alternative ideas allowing you to choose, or to adapt, a visualization approach to suit your own style.

Such skills are not only desirable, of course, but are also transferable, further demonstrating the power and value in the modeling template. Applying the "secrets" of the process should ensure that you acquire *the skill of acquiring skills*—something even more useful than simply improving either your fitness level or your command of public speaking.

You may be wondering why I refer to the process's visible and invisible elements—with their aggregate producing the skill desired—as secrets. The reason is that an expert generally doesn't consciously recognize what goes into their accomplishments; they just perform, often effortlessly. Modeling their methods, however, brings those skills into the realms of conscious awareness, which is where you—and sometimes even the experts themselves—learn *which specifics make the difference*. That's the magic of the experience for both of you. That's the "secret" of the modeling approach to skill mastery!

YOUR TURN, GIVE IT A TRY!
Choose the specific "moment" in the skill set you are targeting, and draft a preliminary process flow. Hint: Use either one of the visual examples provided or create your own flow format.

To summarize, narrowing the process into specific areas of expertise spotlights several important interconnected aspects of the modeling process:

- Knowledge and insights are *most likely* to result from identifying and using a specific "moment in time" with each expert, which you will be selecting next.
- Learning can be accelerated by focusing on a more specialized subject area. Don't be afraid to "dig deep."
- Interconnected activities and micro-moments influence outcomes, even when it's not immediately apparent.
- Gaps in understanding the process, left unresolved, can negatively impact the likelihood of acquiring the desired skill(s).
- Ancillary skill development can be useful with regard to broader developmental objectives.

Chapter 2

Laying the Groundwork for Your First Challenge

Now that you've identified your specific area of mastery, it's time to get started! If you are asking yourself whether or not you need expert help to acquire the skill, then you probably do. Before proceeding, consider a key question: Are you ready to engage with experts yet? None of us want to look foolish or ill-prepared in the eyes of someone we admire. Like any aspect in life, we should be mindful of bringing in expertise only when it is needed. There are two fundamental reasons:

1. We want to use our own finite resources—time and money—wisely.
2. We want to respect an expert's time and goodwill toward us.

Ask yourself:

- How do I know if I need an expert?
- Should I be wary of jumping the gun, or putting the proverbial cart before the horse?

- How will I know that I am ready to start searching for experts?
- What do I need to do to ready myself for the expert search?

If you are not already wondering if you need support, then consider why you haven't been able to achieve the desired skill so far. Your unconscious mind recognizes the need and signals your conscious mind for processing. Through self-reflection, we usually come full circle and recognize the need for additional help. Instinct tells us it is the point when, or shortly after, we exhaust our own bag of tricks and plateau. A classic example is weight loss. A person reaches a plateau after which, no matter what they try, weight doesn't drop. Expert weight-loss intervention opens a new path and places the goal within reach once more. I've seen executives hit similar plateaus looking to perfect public speaking skills, and then unlock progression through professional coaching. The journey begins with recognizing the need for help in acquiring or perfecting a desired skill. The most straightforward way to achieve it is through modeling.

Let's take a moment to consider the 10,000-meter perspective: What is modeling and why bother at all? At its core, modeling is a process of identifying, codifying, and replicating excellence. It provides a toolbox for building almost any life skill—from teaching your child resilience to presenting effectively to a large audience, driving defensively, or selling your services as a consultant.

Several key themes affect modeling outcomes:

- Your own objective assessment of an expert's skill level
- Expert's availability and time commitment
- Expert's openness to exploring the process in detail
- Expert's willingness to be gently focused by the interviewer

- Your personal ability to develop quick connections
- Your own comfort level with an "I don't know what I don't know" attitude

We will start with some best practices for assessing the suitability of an expert before you initiate first contact. In this way, we set the contextual scene before diving into more detail in the next chapter. This will allow you to begin as you mean to go on, with your best foot forward.

ASSESS AN EXPERT'S SKILL LEVEL

An important element in identifying the ideal experts for you to target is to objectively determine where each interviewee is on the proficiency ladder. How will you know if someone you think is an expert is the "real deal"? Firsthand observation or direct experience are the ideal methods, and of course choosing individuals that have something valuable to say in your chosen area (more on this in Chapter 3).

Another question that commonly surfaces is how you share with a "non-expert" (expert-in-training) that they've been chosen in order to provide a contrast to the experts in comparative areas. Everything you choose to say must be true to who you are, as nothing suggests lack of integrity more than saying something simply for the sake of saying it. Here you'll learn to use positive strategies that imply a tacit recognition of each interviewee's current competence level within the target skill without challenging their sense of self.

EXPERT'S AVAILABILITY AND TIME COMMITMENT

Think about how busy your days can be and how highly you appreciate the opportunity, when possible, to manage your day in your own way. Given their tight schedules and many commitments, you'll discover that experts value expectation setting and time management more than most people. In other words, if you propose a sixty-minute meeting then it's your job to keep it to sixty minutes (preferably fifty-five!) in such a way that the expert feels neither rushed nor manipulated.

It's your responsibility to establish a personal rapport. The process tends to work best when the expert chooses the format. Some will prefer a casual social setting (a cup of coffee in Starbucks, a walk, even a golf game) and others something more formal (such as in an office, a meeting room, or perhaps a video conference). Be open to the range of possibilities; it's a vital part of building that connection.

Recognize that unplanned events can, and often do, result in meetings being postponed or canceled. A useful contingency plan is to have more experts lined up than you probably need. This helps you to keep your effort on track and to manage last-minute surprises, thus ensuring the least possible disruption to the schedule.

EXPERT'S OPENNESS TO EXPLORING THE PROCESS

There is an evolutionary step-sequence of learning (Figure 2.1). Running clockwise, the learning continuum starts with unconscious incompetence and ends with unconscious competence.

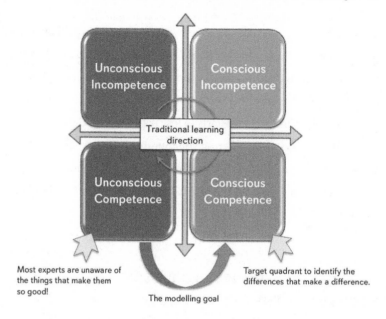

Figure 2.1. Learning continuum.

Experts are generally unconsciously competent. Basically, they are so skilled at what they do that they can accomplish it without actively thinking about it. This phenomenon is sometimes referred to as being on autopilot or being "in flow." During your interviews you may hear comments like "I really don't know how I do it," "Hey, it just happens," or "You know how that works, you'll have done it yourself." This demonstrates the unconscious nature of the skill, challenging you to drill down further until you get to your desired place of knowing.

Throughout the discussion, you'll need to help the expert to bring their knowledge into conscious awareness, using the techniques described in Chapter 5. It will be essential in this phase, particularly if you hear "You'll know what I mean" or something similar, to remain grounded in your own state of *not* knowing. The interview is about their personality, about mapping the world through their eyes. (You'll learn later why influencing the conversation with your personal opinions or experiences is generally unconstructive.)

If an expert unexpectedly starts to lose patience with the discussion, change it up and consider altering your approach. The expert shouldn't feel that it's an inquisition or that the interviewer's agenda is driving the conversation. You will, of course, be leading . . . but it shouldn't *feel* that way!

EXPERT'S WILLINGNESS TO BE GENTLY FOCUSED BY THE INTERVIEWER

Experts will exhibit approaches ranging from the incredibly detailed to quite superficial. Neither extreme is particularly helpful: A balance is your goal. You'll learn to pick up on a phrase, an idea, or a statement, and to choose follow-up questions that will gently guide the conversation in the desired direction without jarring the expert. You might say: "Can we explore this <insert the topic> area a little more?" or "May I ask you a question about <insert the topic>?" (We'll cover these gentle reframing techniques in Chapter 4.)

If an expert operates from an ego-based position (hey, it happens), you can either select another expert or, preferably, choose interview techniques that achieve your desired outcome while respecting the expert's preferred style. Renowned journalists such as Christiane Amanpour, Diane Sawyer, Anderson Cooper, Hu Shuli, and Louis Theroux regularly model how to ask meaningful questions when an expert's or politician's ego, pride, or self-censorship could otherwise get in the way.

YOUR ABILITY TO DEVELOP QUICK CONNECTIONS

Building rapport, the personal connection, sets the tone—for the ease of soliciting information, for the quality of information shared, and particularly for encouraging insights from practical examples. For most people it's a learned skill that assists in every aspect of their personal and professional lives.

It starts when two individuals are in a state of harmony, are comfortable with each other, and feel that they can communicate easily and freely. You'll learn how to appear—and even become—genuinely interested in another person's view (model) of the world, and how to subtly match and pace nonverbal cues.

COMFORT WITH AN "I DON'T KNOW WHAT I DON'T KNOW" ATTITUDE

There are four traits that contribute to effective modeling outcomes: commitment, trust, curiosity, and freedom. Briefly, we need to *commit* to being consciously open-minded, to *trust* in the modeling process to yield the desired outcome, to give ourselves permission to exhibit childlike *curiosity* (the curiosity of "not knowing"), and ultimately to give ourselves permission to *freely* experience whatever lies ahead. It's certain to be new and may be unexpected!

Now, with the journey further outlined, let's explore the details behind the fascinating and mysterious world of modeling techniques and tools to achieve that skill or accomplishment you've always dreamed of.

Chapter 3

Choosing Your Experts

By this point you should be equipped with clarity about the specific skill you want to master, building on the activities you completed in the preceding chapters. The focus now shifts to selecting those individuals to interview from whose input you'll develop a model.

A wise choice of expert sets you on the right path toward mastery. It is worth remembering the saying "garbage in, garbage out"—the individuals chosen as experts collectively form the basis for the knowledge you need for your final skill roadmap. Casual or careless choices might simply set you up for wasting time.

THE TRADITIONAL QUESTIONS

- How do you decide what an expert is, exactly?
- Whom do you choose as experts?
- Where do you find experts?
- How do you "sell" participation in your modeling project to an expert?

- What if your preferred expert says "no"?
- What if an expert backs out of the interview process?
- When should you develop a fallback Plan B?

You may already have experts in mind; perhaps not. In either case, be aware of the two types of experts:

1. Highly rated leaders in the area of focus, lauded for their abilities in the field of concern
2. Experts-in-training: individuals who are sometimes inconsistent in mastery, sometimes perfect in demonstrating the desired skill, at other times just missing the mark

You might wonder how experts-in-training will help you to develop a mastery model when they themselves have yet to fully acquire the desired skills. Great question! This is how: One important element of modeling is identifying the "differences that make a difference." Another way of understanding this idea is being able to recognize the small elements (or differences) that are consistently found in mastery, but not elsewhere. This identification occurs when pinpointing specific behaviors, beliefs, or attributes that consistently produce the desired result. In other words, the experts-in-training can spot—and highlight—the specific behaviors, even when they can't always demonstrate them.

IDENTIFYING EXPERTS

How do you identify the experts you need? Here's an example.

If you want to model speed skating, you'd first have to consider what specific skating skills you might be looking to develop. For instance,

- Do you want to be the fastest skater on the track?
- Do you want to develop your passing technique?
- Do you want to learn how to visualize a race before it happens?
- Do you want to recover from races faster?
- Do you want to learn how to minimize injuries?

Now imagine that you're going to choose a top speed-skating coach from whom to have a single lesson. You determine in advance exactly which issues to explore. If your primary goal is a passing technique, and coach B is the world expert on it, it would be most useful to choose top coach B over top coach A or C. Before learning anything, you first need to be clear about what you're looking to accomplish or achieve.

Another example: running. Usain Bolt is the fastest man on earth (at the time of this writing), holding many world and Olympic titles. However, he is not the fastest runner out of the starting blocks. If modeling a fast track start is your current focus, then your target experts will be those individuals with the fastest clocked starts, not necessarily the fastest track runners.

Compartmentalizing the issues in this way allows identification of best-in-class examples for each micro-moment in the learning process. And the selection matters. If you select mediocrity, you'll model mediocrity. Instead, choose experts that consistently demonstrate the desired result, in whatever precise aspect you have in mind. (Oddly enough, inconsistent but spottily brilliant individuals *can* be the answer.)

Remember, even the most sought-after individuals are often very willing to share their knowledge when approached in the right way. This means if Richard Branson, Usain Bolt, Angelina Jolie, Condoleezza Rice, Jacinda Ardern, or Barack Obama are experts in the skill you seek, you should never be too shy to ask. The best outcome is a "yes" in support of your quest, particularly when it relates to a topic the expert is passionate about. The table below illustrates a couple of examples.

TABLE 1. EXPERT FUNNEL OPTIONS

Desired Skill	Where You Can Look for Experts
Fastest runner out of the blocks	International Olympic team Olympic team trials State, county, or regional teams University athletes (particularly those on athletic scholarships)
Making the perfect *tarte tatin*	Michelin-rated chefs Rosette-rated chefs Culinary schools Cordon Bleu–trained chefs
Delivering the perfect presentation	TED and TEDx speakers Toastmasters Speaking circuit speakers (such as Tony Robbins, Malala Yousafzai, Brené Brown, Nick Vujicic, or Suze Orman) Inspiring leaders in your own organization

At this stage, the question arises of how many experts and aspiring experts to choose for developing a model. Three, five, ten? Even more? A good minimum number if you are looking for a model to develop your own skill is five: three experts and two aspiring/in-training experts. If you want to teach a skill to others, the model will need to be expanded before you do.

Choosing more experts than needed will give you flexibility in the event that an expert backs out of their commitment. Believe me, it happens! This avoids the scramble to find a replacement when—as Murphy's Law predicts—time is short and deadlines loom. Never an ideal situation, this can be proactively managed by building in some fallback choices: a list of seven or eight experts and experts-in-training (consisting of four or five experts and two or three experts-in-training) is generally ideal.

Having determined your target expert, the next question is how to approach and connect with each. Your connection strategy is dictated by the closeness of the existing relationship, if any, with the expert you're after. If the person you want to approach is a stranger, additional introductory steps are probably necessary in order to dramatically improve your chances of their saying, "Yes, absolutely" when you pitch your project.

In my experience, the old-fashioned way—introductions with face-to-face chats—goes a long way toward establishing rapport and accelerating mutual understanding. Such introductions simply tend to work, whether at business conferences, charity events, or social gatherings. The crucial element is that personal connection.

If you'd prefer someone in your personal network to initiate or facilitate the connection, this is probably most easily done through a social networking platform such as LinkedIn, Twitter, WeChat, WhatsApp, Instagram, Facebook, or Meetup.

LinkedIn alone provides several useful options: InMail messaging, a Connect request, or an introduction via an existing first or second network connection. Virtual introductions may be further facilitated using multiperson "hangout" platforms, or with the aid of video chat apps. LinkedIn also boasts the further advantage of a serious, professional, and business-oriented branding: Experts expect to be approached via their profile on the site.

A third-party introduction is most likely to succeed following a chat with your network contact, so she or he needs to properly understand your contact objectives before facilitating the desired connection. In addition, it's critical that the network connection be handled sensitively. Your contact's approach—whether subtle or clumsy—will generally reflect on *you*! For this reason, not only does a thorough briefing matter, but the engagement level of your contact matters too.

With that connection made, we move into the area of your first contact for modeling purposes. Having a clear outline is a must—few things are more off-putting than a contact approach from an unprepared caller. In addition, a high level of advance preparation in itself demonstrates your respect for the expert's time. To put this another way, think about how you felt the last time a colleague seeking advice took up an inordinate amount of time just organizing their thoughts! In short, you must plan *before* sending any email, making any call, or scheduling any meeting.

That crucial initial contact also works best when it's not only personalized but reflective of who you really are. Pretense or bluster adversely impacts on your credibility and can color the entire exchange, even if you later relax. My advice? Be your authentic self in everything you do. If you don't know something, admit it; if you need something, don't be afraid to explain why.

I've experimented with several first-contact methods, with varying degrees of success. My preferred model is a simple expansion on the five Ws[2] (5Ws) of Who-What-When-Where-Why:

- **Where** the first meeting will take place. Agree on a meeting format and location.

---

2   Aristotle, Nicomachean Ethics.

- **WIIFM**[3]: What you hope to get out of your meeting with the expert. Clarity about what's in it for the expert, how they will benefit.
- **What** you're attempting to achieve as a result of it. Clarity about exactly what you are doing.
- **Why** you're attempting to build the modeling roadmap. Explain why you are doing it and how the expert's knowledge will help others (remember, people love to feel valued).
- **When** any outcome needs to be achieved. Be clear on the timeline, time commitment, and what you need from them.
- **How** the experience will unfold for you both. Explaining how the process will unfold and what the expert can expect.

Once the connection is made, the main objective of first contact is to establish clear expectations. Following a brief introduction through the expanded 5Ws (and a little about yourself, where required), the moment arrives to ask if the expert is willing and able to participate in your project. They should by then feel fully briefed, but you should still be clear and up front about the level of time commitment required. It's an important consideration for any participant.

It's common for an expert to decline a participation request purely as a result of scheduling conflicts. It's not personal; it's simply the reality of life reflecting the many roles we each play: spouse, parent, friend, caregiver, leader, teacher, volunteer, whatever. You've done it yourself to others. When it happens to you—and it will—dust yourself off and move on; there are additional names on your expert list for just such contingencies.

In the unlikely event that *several* experts de-commit beyond your

---

3   WIIFM: What's in it for me?

backup list, you'll need to rerun the entire selection process with new individuals. Don't allow yourself to get discouraged; roll with the flow and push on!

To recap (Figure 3.1), by this point you've (a) connected with your experts, (b) delivered a crisp and clear message, (c) finalized your participant list, (d) extended the participant list with fallbacks, in case of unforeseen events, and finally, while hoping this won't be needed, (e) established a contingency plan for your contingency plan.

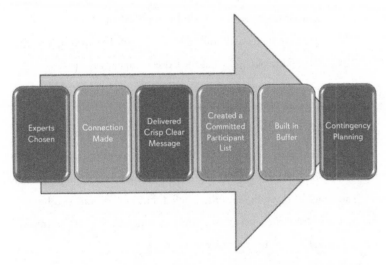

Figure 3.1. Steps leading up to the expert interview.

At last, you can prepare for the initial meeting.

Chapter 4

Preparing to Interview

Here you'll learn how to prepare for the interview in two important aspects: first, enabling your self-confidence to shine through, and second, managing each interview effectively. Preparation involves seven steps:

1. Establishing a meeting time and place
2. Outlining the meeting
3. Recognizing your "chosen moment" process steps
4. Adapting to your expert's needs
5. Making a mental road map of your objectives
6. Organizing your information-collection method
7. Knowing and managing . . . you!

ESTABLISHING A MEETING TIME AND PLACE

This step is perhaps one of the most challenging aspects of any modeling initiative, as your chosen experts undoubtedly juggle tight schedules and numerous competing demands. Flexibility on your part is critical to securing time and a basis for establishing rapport.

Consider the location and format:

- Will the meeting take place in person? If so, where?
- Will it take place via videoconferencing?
- Will it take place via telephone?

You should plan for contingencies, such as a face-to-face meeting being disrupted by travel issues or unforeseen events. Consider adding such follow-up queries as, "How could we reschedule, should this prove necessary?" and "Could a virtual meeting be our backup option?"

Table 2 illustrates some of the main considerations in suggesting and choosing a meeting format.

TABLE 2. ADVANTAGES AND DRAWBACKS OF MEETING FORMATS

Meeting Type	Advantages	Drawbacks
In person	Easier to develop rapport Access to nonverbal cues	Travel time and associated costs Requires a location conducive to intimate conversations and mutual comfort Most susceptible to scheduling disruptions
Videoconferencing	Convenience and comfort (with regard to time and location) Cost-effective Flexible Access to most nonverbal cues	Dependence on broadband Potential for distraction High-quality hardware devices and software required

| Telephone | Convenience and comfort (with regard to time and location) Flexible Cost-effective Allows for freedom of movement | Hands-free device required Most nonverbal cues unavailable Potential for distraction |

There is no single best solution; it's almost entirely situational. Ask your experts how they'd like to connect and what their personal time preferences are. (Some experts tend to choose weekends or evenings, so be prepared to accommodate such requests.)

OUTLINING THE MEETING

Once you have covered our expanded version of the 5Ws (Chapter 3), and you have an agreed-upon time and location, the meeting outline should follow the "PET" model:

- Purpose
- Expectations
- Timeline[4]

A more formal sample outline is shown on the following page, deploying the example of modeling managing nerves connected to public speaking. Of course, if you know the expert on a personal level, your outline will reflect that familiarity. (Note: Nothing in the pre-meeting outline should contain new information. Rather, it should simply summarize the information and issues arising from the first contact meeting.)

---

4   Ken Blanchard, 2001.

PRE-MEETING OUTLINE EXAMPLE

Dear Cynthia,

As discussed, I am currently modeling how experts manage stage nerves in relation to public speaking. The process will include an in-depth evaluation through our discussion of environmental factors (internal and external) that will, I hope, enable us to "draw out" differences in mastery.

We'll initially meet for sixty minutes, dissecting how you manage pre-stage nerves in the context of a successful presentation, speech, play, or other group event. I'll be asking you to cite specific examples from among the many such occasions you've experienced. Afterward, I'll prepare a draft model summarizing the main points, which I'll then run by you in case of any misunderstanding (this should encompass, at most, a half-hour of your time, perhaps ten days after the first meeting).

I'd be more than happy to share the final roadmap model with you, flowing from the idea that "none of us is as smart as all of us."[5] If you'd appreciate this, just let me know.

I'd be most grateful if you could confirm your participation by June 15; I would hope to schedule our initial meeting within the course of the following ten days. The final model is estimated to be completed by July 31, so everything should be finalized by July 25 or so.

Thanks so much for your help, which is greatly appreciated.

Kind regards,

Pratap

---

5   Ken Blanchard, 2001.

YOUR TURN, GIVE IT A TRY!

Create a personal note that reflects you.

RECOGNIZING YOUR "CHOSEN MOMENT" PROCESS STEPS

The third element in the pre-interview phase is knowing and understanding the broad sequence of activities for your chosen moment; in other words, having a general understanding of the end-to-end process. This will encourage greater insights and draw out the very best (sometimes known as unconscious competencies) from your interviewees.

We've all heard such comments as "I just get on stage and start talking; it comes naturally." Though enviable, this tactic is also inherently risky when delivering a keynote speech, for instance. Brilliant presentations, as a rule, don't just "happen." We'll look at the learning-curve concept in detail in Chapter 5, but at this juncture, you may be wondering whether you can get by without a general understanding of the end-to-end process steps. The simple answer is no. Having a command of the relationship between levels of knowledge and depth of thought is essential at this point.

Norman Webb evaluated expectation and assessment tasks, collectively referred to as Webb's Depth of Knowledge (1997). His theory demonstrated that an individual in an extended thinking mode (the highest level) taps into the realms of what else can be done with the knowledge. It's in this mind space that we can sell ideas, devise new ways of achieving, collaborate with multiple individuals, and raise the level of reasoning. This is important to an interviewer, as it demonstrates why our depth of learning from the expert comes when we ask a deep level of thinking and probing questions, in order to tease out innovative answers.

Question quality transcends the basics to consider the how and why it matters. The subtle nuances that emerge from deeper questions tend to produce the "differences that make a difference"—or, in other words, the competencies that the experts just do! A model (Figure 4.1) reflecting the depth of questions and their alignment to mastery highlights the typical frequency with which this occurs throughout everyday life.

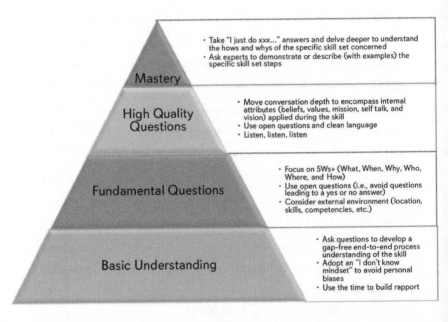

Figure 4.1. Question hierarchy process model.

YOUR TURN, GIVE IT A TRY!

Let's return to our micro-step moment of "Managing Stage Nerves" to apply Webb's theory in practice. Using the skeleton diagram in Figure 4.2, list the basic and advanced questions you think apply in the four quadrants. An answer key is included in the Appendix, allowing you to check your understanding.

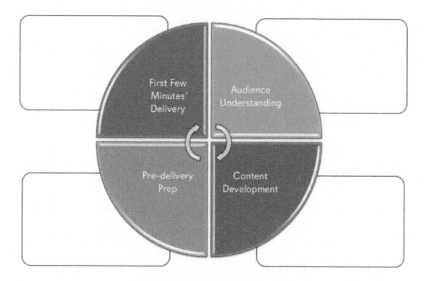

Figure 4.2. Establishing process categories for expert exploration.

YOUR TURN, GIVE IT A TRY!

Take some time to write several key questions that will stimulate the depth of thinking needed to get to the heart of your expert's mastery in the desired skill. These will come in handy soon. (Hint: Use the question hierarchy in Figure 4.1 to help you.)

ADAPTING TO YOUR EXPERT'S NEEDS

Rapport is a key prerequisite to getting quality information from your expert. So, what is rapport? How do you achieve it?

At its most basic level, rapport is a connection between two individuals where each gets a sense (or feeling) of being on the same wavelength—when two people relate well and naturally to each other. Looking at the typical elements present—and in no particular order, because, after all, this is about building a relationship, not ticking off boxes—the requirements include the following:

1. A comfortable location, one that lends itself to an intimate conversation.

2. Thorough pre-meeting preparation. (We each appreciate a discussion where the moderators or interviewers have done their homework and make good use of time. Nobody is crazy about being obliged to spend half the time allotted to explaining things readily accessible on their own website or via social media!)

3. Open-minded questions to kick-start the conversation and deployment of shared phrases, ideas, and concepts (more on this point in Chapter 5).

4. An "I don't know" mindset—avoiding conscious or unconscious personal biases or any attempt at one-upmanship with regard to the expert's own experiences. (It's also good to be clear and open about your intended approach with your interviewee beforehand.)

5. A childlike curiosity and wonder in your conversations: "I'd really love to know more about <the activity moment>." "Tell me, what kind of nerve does it take to launch something like that?"; "How did you decide to do it this way versus any other way?".

6. Being respectful, responsible, reassuring, and recognizing (your

impact on the direction of the conversation). These are the four Rs that make up the major R: rapport. (See Figure 4.4 for greater insight on the 4Rs.) Once an expert feels comfortable with you, the conversation is likely to be of value to both parties!

7. A receptive state of inviting and eliciting information (covered further in Chapter 5) that recognizes and facilitates your interviewee's preferred strategies for doing what they do.

8. A dynamic approach, one capable of being subtly adjusted to any nonverbal feedback received.

You may wonder why rapport—a common, human state of being—requires such in-depth consideration. After all, isn't it a given that the expert will tell me what I need to know? Perhaps the simplest way to answer this question is with an example that we've each experienced at some stage in our lives.

Think back into your past and remember one of those times where you've been grilled by someone about where you were, what you were doing, why you were doing it, or whom you were with. Yes, the old parental/teen inquisition! Well, we were all teens once, and that feeling of being pinned-down or grilled is exactly what we wish to avoid. Rapport is the best way of preventing your expert from feeling it.

You can build rapport through nonverbal, as well as verbal, cues. Whether you agree or disagree with the controversial conclusions of Mehrabian's well-known 1967 nonverbal communication research studies,[6] which suggest the majority of communication is transmitted nonverbally,

---

6   70 percent of communication is body language, 23 percent is voice tone and inflection, and only 7 percent is the spoken word.

is less important than your willingness to recognize *the importance of consistency* between verbal and nonverbal messages.

As an interviewer, you have a responsibility to align what you hear to what you see: posture, limb shifts, speed of breathing, eye contact and movements, skin flushing, language patterns, or anything else that might gift you any personal insight into your interviewee's thoughts or feelings in that moment.

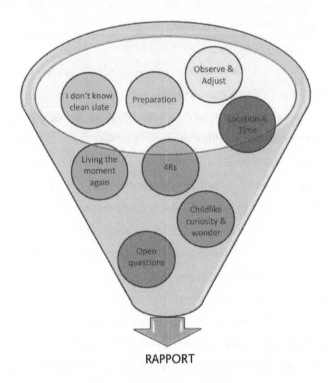

Figure 4.3. Establishing rapport.

Once you've coordinated these eight simple techniques (Figure 4.3), you can relax, open up, and display as much genuine interest as you almost certainly possess. In other words, you can "be your best self on your best day." Good rapport in such circumstances is almost a given.

Next: Have you ever wondered how you come across to other people? Well . . . check! Video your discussion with a volunteer and be as open and candid as you can—you won't learn anything meaningful if you aren't. Then ask for the interviewee's feedback, preferably before watching the video replay.

Questions to explore:

- How was the experience for the other person?
- What did they want to experience more of and what did they especially like?
- What, if anything, would they have liked to experience less of?
- How were the pacing, the timing, and the give-and-take aspects?

Armed with their feedback, watch your replay at least twice: once in normal replay and then again in fast-forward (e.g., 2X or 4X) mode.

What to watch for on normal replay

- Look for any reactions of the interviewee (however subtle: Do they turn aside, half-laugh, look down, or look away?) and then look at yourself. Did you pick up on these and adjust your own behavior or line of questioning?
- Did your expressions show any inappropriate reactions to the interviewee's communication?
- Did you un/consciously "mirror" their body language? (If your interviewee was engaged, did you lean forward or nod, for example?)
- Check for *your* tone, speed, pitch, and language patterns, and for open versus closed questions.

What to watch for on fast-forward replay

- This time, observe your body movements. Are they appropriate to the environment? (For example, large arm gestures work best in a large, open space; small gestures are more telling in a confined space.)
- You and your interviewee should almost seem to be involved in a dance during a fast-forward replay. (If this doesn't happen, however, it doesn't mean that you failed with the connection. It simply provides you with objective feedback from which to finesse your own style.)

Objectively evaluate what you did or didn't do, so you can fine-tune it and feel more connected to the interviewee's personal vibe next time. Keep practicing developing rapport: It will come naturally at some point, and it makes for a richer experience on both sides of the microphone.

Never forget that *you* are the determining factor in whether the expert feels truly respected and valued. Your communication style is what *most* influences the depth of conversational insights achieved (i.e., using a 4Rs style model, shown in Figure 4.4).

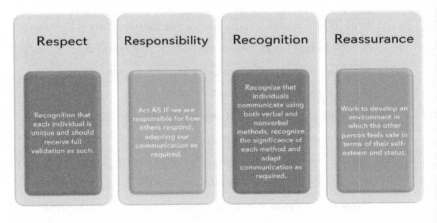

Figure 4.4. The 4Rs model.

The best journalists learn this lesson early on in their careers. It enables them to ask the questions that other journalists dare not attempt. They can ask away with direct and hard-hitting queries because their manner doesn't suggest judgment or threaten their interviewee's assurance or self-esteem. Instead they focus dispassionately on the interviewee's behavior and impact—and not only "live" but even in later commentary or written editorials.

Now *that's* a skill worth modeling!

YOUR TURN, GIVE IT A TRY!
Practice developing rapport with a volunteer, discovering who each other's hero is. Limit your time to six minutes and see how far you get. (Suggestion: video it and watch the replay.)

MAKING A MENTAL ROAD MAP OF OBJECTIVES

Building upon the rapport level you've established, you need a plan of action with two main objectives:

- Getting to the heart of the chosen moment, and
- Providing your expert with the freedom to share their knowledge *their* way

Your interview plan should apportion appropriate weight to both heart and mind levels of explorations within the Personality Map[7] illustrated in Figure 4.5: both are equally critical in model development. The

7   Robert Dilts and Todd Epstein (Logical Levels) 1990, Reg Connolly (Personality Map) 1998.

heart levels (beliefs, values, identity, vision/mission) are the areas we need to access in order to learn the expert's true secret—what makes their skill appear to be so effortless?

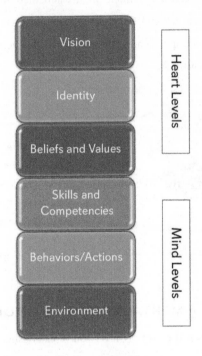

Figure 4.5. The Personality Map.

Your next challenge will be helping your expert to speak in-depth about a specific moment in time, while allowing them sufficient elbow room to segue into related (and potentially still more fruitful) moments. In layperson terms, it's about keeping the expert focused without shoving them into a straitjacket.

Generally, people love to share experiences and are more than willing to talk about themselves—with any luck, through fascinating stories. By using the agreed scope in your meeting outline as a touchstone, you can gently refresh expectations and use it to facilitate a soft reframe should the conversation wind up waterlogged in some unproductive detour. (More on reframing in the next chapter.)

ORGANIZING YOUR INFORMATION-COLLECTION METHOD

A simple, yet effective, information-collection model is one that was originally developed for computing by Miller, Gallanter, and Pibram (1960) and referred to as TOTE (Test, Operate, Test, and Exit). It was updated by Grinder (1979) within the context of Neuro-linguistic Programming as Trigger, Operate, Target, and Exit, and again by Connolly (1998) to TATE (Trigger, Action, Target, and Exit). The method, herein referred to as TATE (Figure 4.6), is the recommended structure to further develop the expert's strategy and process model (and is covered in greater detail in Chapter 5). This framework should ideally be integrated with the six levels of the Personality Map (Figure 4.5) in order to develop a functionally complete model—one factoring in both visible and invisible elements. It offers an intuitive and natural way to identify, step by step, the key elements required to perform the desired skill at an expert level. As a bonus, it produces a clear goal and achievable means by which to attain it.

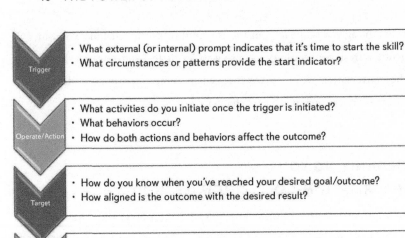

Figure 4.6. TOTE/TATE model.

The TATE system—pure logic—is enhanced when combined with the Personality Map because the map offers a fuller "heart and mind" understanding of the expert concerned. Combining the two should assist you in eliciting and extracting nuggets of genius from your expert. Remember, your objective is to learn how an expert does what they do by

- Understanding their internal behaviors, including beliefs, core values, self-identity, and vision (or mission)
- Examining their external behaviors: what they do, who it's done with, where it happens, and what skills and capabilities are displayed

We start our understanding from the outside and move inward, from the environment level through to the "vision thing." Starting at the external (or mind) levels allows for a level of detachment as rapport develops, and the inner (or heart level) areas remain protected for the expert. The inner level opens up naturally as the level of rapport increases.

To bring this into perspective, think about how defensive you might feel if someone, perhaps a work colleague, suddenly began addressing the most intimate or sensitive areas in your life without having previously made a single effort to form a trusting and respectful relationship with you. This kind of approach can shut down conversations before they have a chance to get going, and can permanently put the kibosh on any serious level of trust (Figure 4.7).

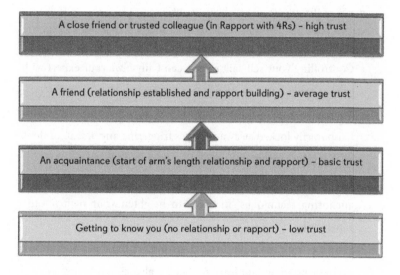

Figure 4.7. Natural trust flow.

The best rule here is to take time and care to establish rapport before exploring more personal spaces. You'll likely get only one opportunity on that day, so . . . take the time you need to get it right.

KNOWING AND MANAGING . . . YOURSELF

The final pre-interview area we need to explore is you! It may seem somewhat counterintuitive, given our emphasis so far, but you are a critical element in steering every interview to a successful outcome.

You've undoubtedly seen a celebrity or world leader interview that was painful to watch—one where either the interviewer or the interviewee lost control of their emotions, resulting in a media car crash. Ouch! Okay, this can make for entertaining TV, but how can you ensure it never happens to you?

The answer is simpler than you might think. It starts with recognizing that, as the interviewer, you're responsible for adapting your style to meet the needs of the expert, never the other way around.

You're also responsible for applying the 4Rs to yourself. This means—

- Controlling your self-talk so you can truly *hear* your expert without your own inner chatter drowning them out.
- Managing your own inner world. You have to ensure that you've temporarily locked away any issues triggering anger, fear, or doubt so that they can't interfere with the success of the process.
- Being the "best you that you can be" on the day: using positive anchoring techniques[8] in order to heighten your own intuitive capabilities.
- Showing humility with an "I don't know" mindset. This process is about listening and learning but it's also about *the expert*, their experiences, their insights, and their knowledge. It's not about you. Without this mindset, you risk wasting their time and your own.
- Feeling and demonstrating respect. Ideally, you can facilitate a level-playing-field atmosphere where two people can connect, to mutual benefit.

---

8   More on this technique using the Circle of Resources and your Panel of Experts in Chapter 13.

Managing yourself also means being responsible for the emotions you show, the words you choose, the behaviors you exhibit, and your own state of mind. You and your expert deserve nothing less.

So far, we've explored seven key interview preparatory steps, all relevant to the quality and depth of the model you'll ultimately develop:

1. Establishing a meeting time and place
2. Outlining the meeting
3. Recognizing your "chosen moment" process steps
4. Adapting to your expert's needs ("knowing" your expert)
5. Making a mental road map of your objectives
6. Organizing your information collection method
7. Knowing and managing . . . you!

By this point we should be in a perfect position to conduct an interview in a way that will extract the greatest value for everyone concerned. Read on!

Chapter 5

Conducting Your Interviews

It's almost showtime; only a few more preparatory steps left! This is a good place to reinforce a critical concept with any interview: It's important to remain focused and work through the process with the interviewee as expeditiously as possible, without the expert feeling rushed. Each participant should ideally share a high-level, positive experience with you. For example, if your interviewee is a last-minute substitution, remember that the person in front of you isn't the one who let you down. Be careful that any latent frustration you might be feeling doesn't seep into your next task. Every participant deserves the best "you" that you can be.

Next, we'll explore ways for you to build a snappier rapport, keep conversations on topic, and appear effortless in doing so. To accomplish this, it's important to keep in mind two important factors:

- Associating the expert with a strongly positive previous experience of applying his or her skill
- Drawing out behaviors that the expert is *no longer consciously aware* that they do

Before getting too far into the interview process, let's think about how people typically learn. So, how *do* people typically learn, anyway? Mostly, we learn in a systematic way (Figure 5.1), starting from a place of not knowing—sometimes even from a place of being *unaware* of not knowing (colloquially, "You don't know what you don't know"). Learning results from evolving from this into a phase of *knowing* that we don't know: the state of "conscious incompetence."

When someone begins to feel comfortable in applying a new skill, a new level of self-awareness (of competence) emerges. This "conscious competence" phase replaces the state of "conscious incompetence."

Once the wished-for skill is fully acquired, we naturally put less conscious thought into doing it. At last, we can demonstrate mastery with ease. This final phase in the learning curve is referred to as "unconscious competence." This is where a true expert's excellence will lie.

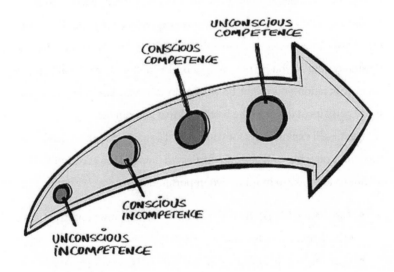

Figure 5.1. Learning competence flow.

Experts are often unaware of the full extent of their mastery. Awareness normally only surfaces through insightful questioning, which can illuminate a rich understanding of the behaviors, skills, capabilities, beliefs, and values necessary to truly excel.

Diagramming the Personality Map's integrated concepts (Figure 5.2) should provide a clearer idea of the systematic approach I recommend. (Tweak the process as needed to make it comfortable for you; keeping the flow authentic is essential to success.)

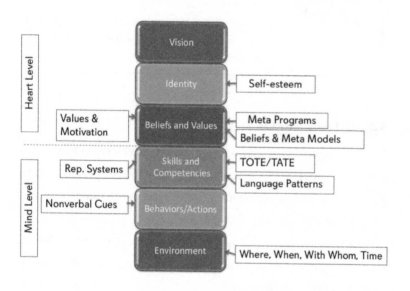

Figure 5.2. Enhanced Personality Map.

To recap where we are: the interviewer (you) and the interviewee (the expert or aspiring expert) are in a comfortable setting and the expert has identified a specific moment where they recall being their "best self," nailing their skill. So, what might represent a typical "moment in time"?

Returning to the example of managing stage nerves, a strongly positive moment in time might involve a recent "on fire" performance before a live audience, when the expert's presentation instigated energy, and he or she triumphantly succeeded in actively engaging their audience.

YOUR TURN, GIVE IT A TRY!
Take a few minutes to select two "on-fire moments" from your own personal experience. Brainstorm possible ideas with a friend or colleague, then share why you chose those particular moments.

BUILDING RAPPORT

The steps required to develop a strong rapport might seem, at first glance, glaringly obvious. Why? Well, you simply do it already, reflected in the fact that you have good friends, great working relationships with colleagues, and strong family relationships. In short, you almost certainly have an "unconscious competence" in terms of building rapport that we need to bring into your conscious mind, enabling you to effortlessly apply these skills in formal situations.

Choose a comfortable setting

- Minimize loud environments, distracting smells or sounds, bright lights, and—as much as possible—the distractions of all those techno buzzes, pings, and rings that can hinder personal connections.
- As any good host would, offer the expert something to drink (the

options are dependent on the time, location, and expert concerned). Alcohol in moderation is rarely an issue; however, too much (surprise!) tends to reduce the quality of the discussion. Also, remember that in some cultures, *any* alcohol at all is inappropriate. It's crucial to familiarize yourself with local customs in order to avoid a faux pas here.

- Choose comfortable chairs. Discomfort is distracting; proactively prevent it.

- Select a day and time that isn't squeezed at both ends between competing priorities. A rushed interview often produces a shallower performance, the predictable result of too many commitments.

Slow down and match your expert's pace

- Slowing down gifts your expert with the ability to remain associated with his or her chosen moment.

- A slower pace also offers the time and space for thinking. Both are critical with regard to quality and depth of experience.

- Matching your interviewee's pace and tone facilitates a more personal encounter, laden with rich insights. (Of course, this might mean that you're towed along very swiftly indeed . . .)

- Consider how guarded *you* might feel if you experienced a "disconnect" with the person exploring an aspect of your life. Now recall one of the many times your personal barriers were lowered and you felt secure and seen—a feeling that often ends in the formation of new friendships. That's the rapport that we're after: the matching of tone, pacing, body language, level of engagement, and overall receptiveness.

Use unbiased language (a.k.a. clean language)

- Unbiased language is about asking open and nonleading questions.
- Open questions seek information rather than a yes or no answer. For example: "Are you going to Deb's tonight?" elicits a "yes" or a "no." Rephrasing this as an open question—"What are you planning to do tonight?"—gives the option for more information. ("I thought I would drop in on Deb tonight, in case Chris might be there. I want to check in with him on the new sponsorship deal.")
- Open questioning also implies a nonleading and unbiased approach. For example: "Do you really like that new guy in sales, Lichen?" has a suggestive undertone, in that you might think Lichen a bit "off." A nonleading opening might be: "What do you think of the new guy, Lichen?" This implies that you're simply interested in gaining information.

Use the expert's own words to clarify and to frame follow-up questions. If the expert refers to something as a problem, you can ask, "Why might this prove to be a problem, in your experience?" Otherwise, try something along the lines of "What effect could implementing XYZ have?" Note that you're not suggesting anything. The language is completely neutral.

Getting back on track from a conversational detour

It is not uncommon for a conversation to go off on a tangent or take a slow winding road. While it may be frustrating at times, there are seamless ways to steer it back on track. So, how can you reset the conversation course? Try one of these methods:

- Clarify exactly how the story being told actually connects with the moment being modeled. There may be some connection you're unaware of. Remember, if you were the expert, you'd be the interviewee. Alternatively, there may be no useful link, in which case you can gently steer the conversation back to the topic at hand.

- Take the excuse of the shared story to frame a new directional question—one that tilts the interview back toward your particular area of interest.

Matching body language

- Your task here is to match—but *not* to mimic—your expert's body language. For example, if the expert is leaning back in a relaxed manner then you'll want to appear similarly in command. If you seem to be rigidly upright while the expert is almost slouching, the mismatch adversely impacts rapport. If your expert's arms are physically expressive, you could respond similarly, though perhaps more discreetly. Because overtly mimicking can appear disrespectful, the safest bet is to gently vary your movements within a slightly more reserved or narrow range.

- Be conscious of their breathing patterns and physical movements, which can be extremely telling. If a question startles your interviewee, they might sit up sharply or uncross their legs, for example. Similarly, a lack of eye contact might suggest unease, shyness, nerves, fatigue, or boredom.

Understand physical reactions (representational systems)

- Eyes matter. There are books on the meaning of eye movements, though these can be contradictory: The meaning behind various behaviors are, at times, unique to the individual. However, if your interviewee taps a foot or their eye-movement speed changes, they are likely to be feeling *something*—whether impatient, excited, engaged, or stressed. Your observations will gradually allow you to establish insight into the expert's moments of thought, hearing, visualization, and feeling.

- Observe body movements using a soft-filtered view, a subtle observational approach rather than one of overt inspection. The phrase you might have heard as a child applies: "It's rude to stare!" Observational subtlety and quiet receptivity are critical when interviewing, especially when nonverbal cues might suggest that the expert is engaged in taxing internal activity, such as thinking, in one way or another.

- Their tone of voice can also be telling. When a recollection is enjoyable, their tones will generally be slower, lower, and more relaxed. If the association is stressful, then the timbre could seem harsher, higher, and possibly curt.

Motivation and attitude (language patterns)

- Does the expert value sameness or differences in their world? In other words, are predictable processes preferred to significant changes in routine? Consider exploring how these attitudes might relate to their mastery.

- Does the expert deploy motivators in their process? If you hear statements like "I want . . ." it generally indicates a moving toward something motivational, whereas "I don't want . . ." is a move away from something motivational. Consider how different motivational styles might impact your interviewee's abilities (and even their career). Imagine that you hear the following in a leadership meeting: "When we updated the company's pension plan from defined benefit to defined contribution, employees rebelled en masse, so I never want to initiate another HR transformation change again!"

This is an example of an away-from motivator, something that the speaker wants to well and truly distance themselves from.

- Does the expert tend toward a more rigid thinking style (controller) or a more flexible style (adapter)? What specific capabilities, beliefs, or types of identity make it easier to excel at the particular skill involved?

- Does the expert use their own internal reference system for feedback, or are external sources of feedback or advice solicited? (Internal referencers tend to lead with "I know . . ." whereas external referencers require feedback asking "What do you think . . .")

To sum up rapport

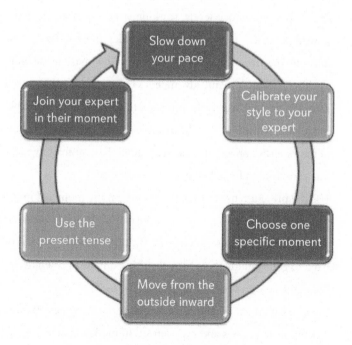

Figure 5.3. Getting into rapport within the expert's chosen moment.

Create rapport through a few simple steps:

1. Slow your (speaking) pace and soften your voice. This combination encourages comfort and relaxation in others.

2. Calibrate with your expert's pace of breathing, eye movements, body movements, and speed. Note the expert's normal range as a baseline for any changes that might occur during your discussion together.

3. Give your interviewee the time and space needed to select a specific moment when they were masterfully executing the skill you've chosen to model. Remember, *it must be a strong and positive memory* so they can relive it in rich detail with you, as if it were occurring right now.

4. Guided by the Personality Map (Figure 4.5), gently move through the six building-block levels, working your way from the outside inward (from the mind levels to the heart levels, or you can think of it as moving from the visible attributes to the invisible attributes). Pushing forward too quickly impedes rapport and, when extreme, can even damage trust, which is sometimes difficult to reestablish. Judge your tempo at the "heart level" based on your assessment of the expert's nonverbal cues. Remember: Discomfort is generally first displayed in body language.

5. Use the present tense to keep the expert "in the moment" in order to provide the most meaningful information possible. Accidental slips into the past tense can disrupt the flow. If this happens, you'll need to gently guide them back (by using only the present tense in your language and remaining relaxed yourself).

6. Identify with them in their associated state, meaning be authentic in sharing their feelings and experiences. In modeling, this step is the

culmination of rapport and crucial for connection. Think about one of those times when you and a friend shared a fantastic and adventurous experience; it was that sharing that created the bond that will always exist between you. The same can be true in your interview—and, when it is, the most powerful work can be accomplished!

In terms of rapport, the 4Rs are essential:

1. **Respect:** Respect the individual themselves.
2. **Recognition:** Recognize nonverbal cues and adapt (mirror nonverbal cues but do not mimic).
3. **Reassurance:** Ensure that you're fostering a safe place to be open.
4. **Responsibility:** Own the other person's response toward you. (Note: We don't actually own their behaviors or feelings. Use this framework to remain consciously aware of your impact on others.)

YOUR TURN, GIVE IT A TRY!
Practice developing rapport in formal situations from now on. For instance, the next time you are at a conference, at a grocery store, or picking up a coffee, connect with one or two new people with casual small talk (such as asking them how their day is so far). Does it feel effortless yet?

Now you're equipped with rapport skills to connect with each expert. So, your next step is exploring the interview process itself.

EXPLORING HOW IT'S DONE

Mind levels (externally oriented elements)

Extending the enhanced Personality Map framework (Figure 5.2), we'll now explore both the practical and systematic aspects of the interview. This section expands on each of the Personality Map building blocks in turn, and is designed to help you perform as effortlessly as possible during an interview.

Environment is the first building block, designed to relate the surroundings and conditions within which the skill is being displayed. The questions typically start with "Where is," "Who is," "What is," or "When does X happen?"

Using "managing stage nerves" as a template, environmental questions about the event may include the following:

- Where is your presentation taking place?
- Who might be attending?
- What time of day is it?
- How long have you been preparing for the moment you're now inhabiting?
- What audiovisual equipment is being used?
- How long is the event scheduled to last? (Note: *Never* overrun!)

You'll notice that the present tense is used throughout, emphasizing the expert's association with their chosen moment. If you inadvertently ask "Who was attending your presentation?" instead of "Who is attending your presentation?" don't worry. Simply recognize your slight slip, remain relaxed, and continue, returning your choice of tense to the present. You'll know if the expert has disassociated from or reassociated with their chosen moment because of their own choice of tense. You'll hear, for example, "There is . . ." (associated) to "There was . . ." (disassociated), or "I am . . ." (associated) to "I was . . ." (disassociated). Normally, though, the interviewee will take their cue from you.

But . . . why does tense matter?

It matters because memories represent a static and filtered recollection of events, whereas reliving the moment goes far deeper, offering more vivid detail and intuitive recollection where the senses are re-experiencing the event. The nuances, hidden behaviors, and small details can be critical with regard to identifying consistent expert traits. Seemingly tiny things, often left unconsciously processed, can be unearthed when the moment is relived.

This reliving technique is so potentially powerful that police officers and detectives routinely use it to help crime victims recollect details previously forgotten or suppressed. In the right hands, it can make the difference between a conviction and an unsolved crime.

Behaviors/
Actions

The second building block, behaviors and actions, explores the expert's visible signals and activities.

You'll need to observe:

- Breathing (rate and pace)
- Posture (how are they sitting, standing, walking)
- Muscle usage (which muscles are active or relaxed)
- Manifestations of stress or anxiety (palpitations, perspiring, restlessness, sweating, etc.)
- Physical actions (crossing arms or legs, eye contact, laughter, etc.)

Some skills may involve unconscious body movements—such as how a chef's shoulder rolls when whipping ingredients—so make a note of this fact. Later on, you will need to determine if these unconscious movements are meaningful differences impacting skill aptitude.

You can also consider habits, quirks, or routines idiosyncratic to that individual, such as a professional athlete with a lucky pair of socks that they believe actually influences their ability at the 400-meter hurdles. Clearly a genuine belief for the athlete concerned, it's equally clear that it has no impact on the beliefs and therefore skill of any other person. (Sadly, I'm not going to become an elite hurdler simply by borrowing a top hurdler's "lucky" socks!)

Another example might involve cabinetmaking. A master cabinetmaker's technique, in terms of body posture, hand feel, or arm angle, represents observable physical excellence. When the expert, during an interview, relives the moment, you might observe this unconscious physical movement replicated. (This is even likelier when watching the expert live in action—always an ideal choice where practical.)

The third and final external building block seeks to establish and understand the overall skills and competencies used during the performance of the skill. During your discussion you'll notice several clues that identify the patterns the expert prefers. (Hint: Patterns can change in between conversational moments; be alert for it.)

Language and thought patterns

Be aware of the expert's language patterns and patterns of thought:

- What words or phrases does the expert tend to use?
- Are absolute words (such as always, never, absolutely, completely, or definitively) favored or preferred?
- Is responsibility assumed? Or blame deflected?
- Is the expert drawing meaning from the actions of others (without explicitly verifying their intent)?
- Does the expert make broad or sweeping statements?
- Are there assumptions surrounding something always being or never being possible?
- Is information being omitted (such as when describing how something is occurring)?

Also, representational (rep) systems can help you determine *how* the expert is processing information at that moment. For example, what's the expert's preference with regard to how experiences (or things) are processed? Visual, auditory, kinesthetic, auditory digital?

- Visual: "I see . . ."
- Auditory: "I hear . . ."
- Kinesthetic: "I feel . . ."
- Auditory digital: weighting facts and figures versus inner chatter (inner chatter being internal self-talk)

(Hint: What you learn here can help you to identify other areas of potentially fruitful exploration.)

In addition to the Personality Map, the TATE model (which we cover in more detail later in this chapter) offers other useful methods for you to explore with your expert at this point.

Skill process steps (the target achievement path)

- This involves leveraging a structural model to identify and analyze activities involved in end-to-end performance of the skill.

Techniques (which the expert applies to perform)

- What competencies are used to carry out the skill concerned?
- How were the competencies developed? (For example, through research, trial and error, training, shadowing a master expert, or something else?)
- What's the best work-based advice the expert ever received?

YOUR TURN, GIVE IT A TRY!
Practice remaining in rapport when dealing with an uncooperative individual. (Role play with a friend or colleague.)

Once you have a complete picture of these three aspects, you're ready to transition from the visible (mind-based) attributes to the invisible (heart-based) ones in order to elicit the expert's internally generated elements of skill mastery.

Heart levels (internally oriented elements)

Before we start this section, remember that this "inside out" part of the journey is one that only a privileged few ever experience. With that privilege comes responsibility to be thoughtful, generous, and kind to your interviewee.

First, let's explore beliefs, values, and motivation.

Beliefs and
Values

Think of yourself as a sponge, capable of internalizing every element of the interview being experienced. Or imagine that you're learning from every angle: from hearing, seeing, feeling, and in some cases, even touching or tasting (the latter two when modeling physical skills, such as dragon boat racing, golfing, or cooking).

Being open to everything allows us to reach a depth of knowledge rarely attained otherwise. Your personal approach through the three heart-level elements—more than almost anything else—can set the tone for the quality of the interview achieved. It might be both easier and harder than you think!

First, identify the personal areas you can explore with your experts.

1. **Motivation:** Determine what drives the expert to do what they do, and why it works.

Questions to consider exploring:
   a. Are you being pulled toward achieving a defined goal? Or could you be pushing yourself away from something undesirable?
   b. How does this motivation help or hinder your process or outcome?
   c. How does your internal or external motivator impact the process or outcome? (Recall: internal = self-motivation, external = motivated by others)

2. **Values:** Understand which of the expert's values come into play when doing "their thing."

Question:
   a. How do your personal values relate to your motivation and beliefs?

3. **Beliefs:** Identify how the execution of the expert's skill(s) demonstrates their core beliefs.

Possible queries:
   a. How do your beliefs play into your actions and behaviors as you perform?

b. Which beliefs hinder a successful outcome, in your view?

c. How do you build belief in your ability *before* expertise is consistently manifesting?

4. **Self-talk:** Comprehend the impact that the expert's self-talk has on their ability to do the skill in question.

Helpful questions:

a. How does your (positive or negative) self-talk impact the process and its outcome?

b. How do you manage negative self-talk before and during performance?

c. How does positive self-talk assist you before and during performance?

d. What kind of self-talk happens after the performance?

All of us occasionally draw upon a filtering approach, especially when being pressed about our core values and beliefs. There are three particularly relevant categories of filters:

1. Ignoring
2. Generalizing
3. Distorting

As an interviewer, you need to be alert to these filters so that you can gently disentangle the expert from them where needed. By disentangling, you will understand how the expert analyzes, builds, and develops the rules and constraints they apply to themselves.

Table 3 covers common filters and how they tend to manifest themselves.

TABLE 3. INFORMATION-PROCESSING FILTERS

Filter Category	Filter Type	Signs to Look For
Ignoring	Missing information	Any kind of missing information; the process as explained by the expert doesn't quite hang together
	Fuzziness	Lack of clarity about people, places, or things
Generalizing	Sweeping statements	An expressed opinion based on very few data points or examples that support the opinion
	Impossibilities	A belief that something is not achievable for him or herself or others; frequently lacks logic in support of the belief
	Self-imposed rules	Expressing information in terms of what he or she must do or expects others to do
Distorting	Not owning opinions	Hiding behind others to express an opinion ("people believe . . . some people say . . .")
	Extrapolating ("poor me syndrome")	Exaggerating by attributing one's own feelings to outside events, circumstances, or people
	Reading minds	Making unverified assumptions about others ("you know what I mean . . . they know what I mean")
	Attaching meaning without evidence	Attributing arguments to others without bona fide justification for doing so ("He missed our meeting because he doesn't think I'm important enough...")

Identity

The second element in the heart level (the fifth element in the Personality Map) is identity. Identity relates to how an individual sees him- or herself: the aggregate of values, beliefs, motivations, capabilities, skills, and behaviors.

Identity questions to explore with regard to modeling:

- What are you thinking just before or just as you start the activity?
- What is your inner voice doing or saying?
- How are your thoughts changing as you perform the skill?
- How are your thoughts influencing (hindering) your success?
- How does success look/feel to you?
- How are your feelings (a kinesthetic experience) interwoven with your thoughts (an intellectual experience)?
- How do you monitor your success as you are performing?
- What signals you that you might be missing your mark as you are performing?
- Which of your values are being fulfilled in this process?
- Where is your motivation coming from? (Hint: toward or away from something and internal instead of external?)
- Which thoughts are helping you to achieve success during your moment in time?
- How does how others see you align with how you'd *like* them to see you?

The idea behind exploring this entire topic is to obtain a privileged insider's view of the invisible thoughts bolstering the visible mastery.

Observable skills and activities are straightforward enough to learn; the real secret to excellence is understanding the hidden attributes that are also required.

Again using "managing stage nerves" as our go-to illustration, being a masterful public speaker involves far more than simply walking onstage and delivering a well-scripted message. Instead, it's about walking onstage and delivering a well-scripted message with passion, conviction, energy, inspiration, integrity, and humor, thereby providing something valuable and memorable to those in attendance. To do so requires that you—

- Manage your own frame of mind and self-talk
- Read your audience expertly throughout
- Connect with and communicate your message with clarity and panache
- Adapt to changing conditions

These nuances matter because self-esteem, self-image, and self-confidence all directly and powerfully impact on skill proficiency. In short, talent is a combination of what is visible on the outside *and* what's going on *inside*.

The final element for us to explore is the big picture, or vision.

The vision (or mission, choose the term that resonates most with you) is the life driver within each of us. It's akin to a compass that consciously and unconsciously guides our decisions and actions in life. Within a long-term time scale, vision includes life goals, dreams, aspirations, our personal "calling."

The challenge, in terms of modeling, involves gleaning insights about vision from each chosen expert.

Thought-provoking questions can help to kick-start the process:

- "Of all the important things in your life, which two stand out as the most important for you?"
- "How would you sum up your mission in life?"
- "How does this particular activity or skill help you to fulfill your aspirations?"
- "How does it contribute to or benefit the lives of others?"
- "How would you like to be remembered when you hang up your spurs?"

With these questions, you're looking for patterns—patterns between those elements required to master any particular skill and elements important to the expert but not necessarily required for mastery (idiosyncrasies). As illustrated earlier, lucky socks might make a difference to a particular athlete's pre-race state without being remotely helpful to someone seeking similar success. Wouldn't it be amazing if we could simply wear Usain Bolt's or Florence Griffith Joyner's lucky socks or shoes and become the fastest man or woman in the world? A nice dream, however . . . we need to stay focused on those "differences that make a difference."

It helps if you cultivate the curiosity that came so naturally to you as a child. Remember those kinds of questions you asked your parents? ("Why is the sky blue?" "Why do we always take the back way to Grandma's house?" "Why do trees have to lose their leaves?") Basically, asking is how you learned just about anything . . . until you expanded your circle of reference to include teachers, friends, and the Internet (it's even where you first learned how to separate fact from "fake news" as a very young child).

The point is to remain curious, open, and unbiased; judgment can have no place in your expert discussions. That way, the information obtained (and later aggregated) should form a strong foundation for the First Draft Model (covered in Chapter 6).

YOUR TURN, GIVE IT A TRY!
Practice exploring vision with a friend or family member: What ignites their fire/passion day to day? Or, when all is said and done, how would they like to be remembered? (Hint: Always practice sensitive topics for the first time with someone you trust.)

Once the Personality Map is complete, extend it by exploring the micro-moments (sub-steps) you might need to use to tease out the detail on the day. It's this combined output from the Personality Map and TATE framework that produces your First Draft Model.

Target achievement path

Many roads lead to Rome, but some are shorter, quicker, or better-maintained than others. As covered in Chapter 4, the target achievement path I've found most effective for modeling purposes, mainly for its simplicity, is the TATE model that we will now explore more deeply. I have to acknowledge, here and now, that the process of breaking down any skill (or activity) into intermediate parts is not particularly sexy, so hang in there as we work through this dry but crucial topic.

TATE answers four strategic questions:

1. How do I know when to begin doing <the activity>?
2. What should I be doing once <the activity> starts?
3. How do I know when I've achieved (or completed successfully) <the activity>?
4. What do I do once it's completed?

So, how does TATE work? Returning to our "cooking a perfect omelet" illustration, here's an example of a single step:

Trigger/Test: Check the omelet, is it cooked?

Action/Operate: No: Then leave it a while longer.

Target/Second Test: Check again, is it cooked now? Yes, it is! (A "No" would return us to the Action/Operate stage, leaving it to cook a little longer.)

Ending/Exit: Take it off the stove.

Contrast this simple example with the more complex one of "managing stage nerves." We will concentrate on the moment in time when the speaker has just arrived at the podium to start speaking:

Trigger/Test: Is the audience settled and ready for me?

Action/Operate: Yes: Start with my opener (story, joke, provocative statement). No: Rouse the audience's attention, perhaps with an impromptu "Good morning/afternoon ladies and gentlemen (folks), is everyone comfortable and ready to begin?"

Target/Second Test: Check again, is the audience settled and ready now? Yes: Move on to the next step. No: This would return us to the Action/Operate stage, focusing the audience on you.

Ending/Exit: Continue on energetically with the next part (step) of the rehearsed presentation.

As we've seen throughout these pages, there are several possible questions that can be used to elicit the desired information from experts at each stage (or micro-step of the skill). The extent and depth of questions, of course, correlate with the complexity of the chosen skill.

STEP 1: TRIGGER

The objective in the first step is to gain a deeper understanding of exactly how the expert knows when to begin the moment in time task. This starting element often defines the rest of the process. For this reason, taking enough time to understand the environment within which it happens is important.

Possible questions:

- What is the catalyst suggesting that you need to do this? (people, places, events, feelings . . .)
- What triggers the behavior to start?
- What drivers tell you to stop a previous activity and start this one?
- What's the draw or appeal for you?
- What would happen if you didn't recognize the trigger signs and didn't start the process?

STEP 2: ACTION

You may feel that this is getting a bit obvious. (The trigger for starting a presentation is audience readiness, whereas for starting to create an omelet it is probably that you are simply hungry.) However, our goal here is to dig beneath the obvious, just as we did with the Personality Map, in order to understand the invisible thoughts, feelings, beliefs, and actions in each micro-moment that work together to produce the consistent expertise.

Possible lines of inquiry:

- How are you behaving during the process?
- What are you feeling and thinking?
- What are the steps after the first trigger action? (For example, what's next, then what is next, and then after that, and so on.)
- How are you ensuring that your actions are aligned with your objectives? (How do you know you'll achieve the desired target?)
- How clear is your target outcome? (Is the objective clearly defined or it is more of a vague concept?)
- What clues indicate that your actions are on track?
- How do you know whether to keep going or to stop?
- How often and how do you check your progress throughout the process against the desired objective? (What feedback mechanisms apply?)
- How do you feel if you are not achieving your desired outcome after each micro-moment?
- How do you manage your self-talk when your outcome falls short?
- What steps do you take to modify your behavior(s) if it's not working out?

STEP 3: TARGET

This third test step in the TATE model relates to completion. Simply put, you want to know how the expert knows when they've hit the mark!

Sample questions:

- How do you know when you need to stop doing this activity? (What signals, events, feedback, or thoughts tell you to move on?)
- How do you know if you've completed the actions satisfactorily or unsatisfactorily?
- How do you ensure that your feedback indicators are reliable?
- How do you respond if you are not yet complete?
- How do you respond if you determine that you are?

STEP 4: EXIT

How the process or skill ends is almost as important as its execution, probably because it's the last experience individuals are left with.

Areas of exploration:

- What next, after you've achieved your goal?
- When and how do you reflect on your process experience?
- What is your self-talk throughout?
- How does your self-talk differ, depending upon results?
- How is each experience incorporated into your own personal development?
- Do you celebrate each success or simply and quickly move on to new activities?

You might be thinking at this point: *Why are all these steps worth all the time and trouble that they take?* Because you can only hope to replicate an expert's success through a deep understanding of relevant external and internal elements, and the deeper you drive into them, the more you learn.

For example, Table 4 applies the TATE model to the example of public speaking, specifically the first two minutes of a public speaking engagement (using excerpts from actual interviews with experts and experts-in-training).

TABLE 4. FIRST TWO MINUTES OF PUBLIC SPEAKING TARGET ACHIEVEMENT MODEL

Steps	Similarities between experts and experts-in-training	Differences between experts and experts-in-training
Trigger	An external factor initiates the presentation—customer events, humanitarian causes, educational obligations, employee events, etc.	Ways of managing the "in-the-moment nerves" surrounding speaking publicly range from positively using the adrenaline rush of wanting to "be the best me I can be" (experts), to experiencing anxiety/fear and even full-on panic (more common in experts-in-training)
Action	Engaging audience interaction (approachable style, quips, humor, lively energy) Honoring audience knowledge and intelligence (choosing a communication style that values and respects attendees) Reading nonverbal cues and adapting the message (anticipating thought-provoking questions or prompting reflection)—similar behaviors but at significantly different skill levels	Using tone and pitch to influence audience perception (Hint: Experts generally use a lower vocal tone that projects strength and confidence, encouraging a perception of greater credibility) Internal comfort during presentation (experts) versus internal scrambling (experts-in-training) Using techniques to establish rapport with the audience, effortless appearance (experts)

continued

Target	Using body language in order to achieve rapport (smiles, nods, eye contact) Using behavioral feedback assessed through the depth and quality of questions asked of the speaker (this assumes the venue is conducive to Q&A and/or input)	Continuously assessing nonverbal cues and adapting delivery in response (experts)
Exit	Managing audience reaction (verbal and nonverbal cues, knowing when to conclude . . . a lost art!) Seeking audience input (afterward)	Assessing learning via the audience (typically one-to-one or in small groups post-session) (experts)

YOUR TURN, GIVE IT A TRY!

Practice by creating a TATE model for delivering a thought-provoking twenty-minute presentation on "how artificial intelligence will change lives" (harder challenge), for "making the perfect apple pie" (easier challenge), or choose your own skill.

Conducting successful interviews depends on understanding these five key concepts:

1. The importance of rapport and how to develop and maintain it
2. How the Personality Map (PM) may be used to get an "outside-in" look at how an expert masterfully performs

3. The types of questions most likely to elicit relevant information from experts for subsequent use in the first draft model

4. The TATE model: A useful and structured method for organizing the skill process

5. An applied example of a TATE model (using excerpts from "the first two minutes of a public speaking engagement" template)

Our next step: Integrating all the information gathered from the experts into a first draft model.

Chapter 6

Developing a First Draft Model

S o, here you are, poised with your stack of notes, or your app with annotated notes, or digitally recorded files (such as MP3, MP4, or others) from each interview. What comes next?

The goal is to integrate the interview notes into a crisp and practical draft model. It's often easier to work backward rather than forward, so start with the end in mind. You need to create the model with a view to ensuring you are inherently addressing the following basic questions or objectives:

1. **What** are you seeking to achieve (or help others to achieve)?
2. **Who** are you doing it for?
3. **Why** does it matter?
4. **How** do you plan to organize the process steps?

Let's return to the public speaking example.

WHAT (ARE YOU SEEKING TO ACHIEVE)?

- Help others overcome the fear of public speaking. (Glossophobia, the technical name for the fear of public speaking, is the most common social phobia.)
- Show them how to harness stage nerves (or pre-stage jitters) into a positive energy.

In this skill example, we need to consider the process starting from the initial request to speak at an event, through the first couple of minutes of the presentation itself. In this process timeline, we focus on how experts manage their nerves (or fear). We do so by combining the Personality Map and the TATE models together in order to—

1. Capture the common foundational elements
2. Highlight the differences that make a difference

WHO (ARE YOU DOING IT FOR)?

The model is geared for anyone—

- hoping to overcome glossophobia
- wishing to get into public speaking
- wanting to perfect their existing public speaking skills, whether for career or personal reasons

WHY (DOES IT MATTER)?

Many aspects of our lives require speaking publicly (from business events and wedding speeches to award acceptances and charity fundraisers). Most professionals need to develop this skill.

HOW (DO YOU PLAN TO ORGANIZE YOUR PROCESS STEPS)?

The information is organized in three simple steps.

1. Color-code the information obtained via the Personality Map (PM) and TATE model.

   Blue: Lead-up prep (preparatory steps required before the speaking event)

   Green: Preparatory steps just before beginning your speech (the short period immediately before starting to deliver any presentation)

   Orange: The first minute or two of the presentation itself

2. Aggregate the data (information).

3. Organize it into relatable and teachable activities.

Your choice of medium might entail using a whiteboard (or whiteboard sheets). Other productive options include tablet note-taking apps (two great apps are Notability ©Gingerlabs or OneNote ©Microsoft Corp.), or else audio-video files in MP3 or MP4.

Although these are my preferred methods, adapt as needed to suit your own preference or style. Regardless of what works best for you, once your notes are organized, I strongly recommend that you deploy an 11 x 3 table (Table 5) to capture the commonalities and differences[9] within the PM and TATE models.

---

9   A definition for commonalities and differences, in the context of modeling, is included in the Glossary.

TABLE 5. COMMONALITY AND DIFFERENCE
INFORMATION CAPTURE

	Commonalities	Differences
Vision		
Identity		
Beliefs and Values		
Skills and Competencies		
Behaviors		
Environment		
Trigger(s)		
Action(s)		
Target		
Exit		

To help you organize the notes in your table, a couple of hints are given below. (At this stage you want to avoid filtering information. Simply capture it in the appropriate table category.)

Commonality: Group commonly identified attributes performed at a consistent level in the Commonalities column and note performance differences within the skill in the Differences column. For example, let's say all interviewees use eye contact. The experts-in-training do it a quarter of the time, however. Note this in the Commonalities column as: eye contact is maintained 25 percent of the time. The experts consistently do it all the time; note this in the Differences column as: eye contact is maintained 100 percent of the time. Later on, organize further and analyze to determine if the differences noted are significant or relevant.

Difference: Differences that are unusual features or quirks (idiosyncrasies) should be tagged, as they will be excluded from the finished model. For example, experts wear their lucky socks during each competitive event. The tag could be as simple as: Experts wear their lucky socks during each competitive event [Idio].

MAPPING THE MODEL

With the commonalities and differences laid out in plain view, it's easy to create a clear and meaningful map of commonalities (CORE) and the differences that make a difference (DMD). Ideally, this activity should be completed for each element of both the Personality Map (PM) and TATE model. As a quick reminder, here they are:

1. Environment
2. Behavior
3. Skills and Competencies
4. Beliefs and Values
5. Identity
6. Mission and Vision
7. Trigger(s)
8. Action(s)
9. Target
10. Exit

Figures 6.1 and 6.2 illustrate two of the ten elements: "Actions" and "Beliefs and Identity" from the TATE and PM, respectively. The graphic shows an example of interview information captured from experts. (Some editing may be necessary at this stage, for example where identical or near-identical comments are made by two or more interviewees.)

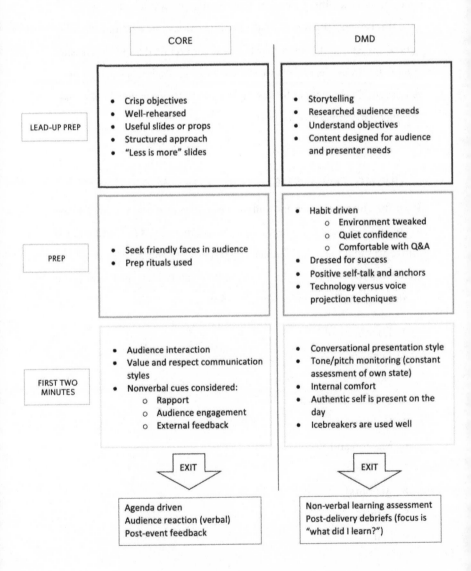

Figure 6.1. Actions—draft interview results (TATE).

The "Actions" map (Figure 6.1) captures the lead-up activities through the first 120 seconds of delivery. Here, the focus is on capturing points without filtering characteristics, such as idiosyncrasies, relevant to only one individual. You will also benefit by grouping common themes among interviewees. For instance, the theme of "structured approach" was described variously by interviewees:

- "The slides have a structured opening, body, and conclusion focusing on . . ."
- "We (the team and I) are coordinating and structuring the delivery in a format that . . ."
- "A formal agenda is ready; the stage is set which lays out a defined roadmap for . . ."
- "The course curriculum is clarified; the content is developed using a methodical format to . . ."

A similar process was followed for the "Beliefs & Identity" element of the Personality Map (PM), illustrated in Figure 6.2.

	CORE	DMD
LEAD-UP PREP	• I can't please everyone • Overriding desire to share/teach or reassure	• Boost team = boosting oneself • Generate ideas/discussion • No resting on laurels (arrogant to do so)
PREP	• Be oneself • Feedback is important	• Outcome okay = trust yourself • Crisp opener and closer belief • Delivery matters • Lose ego • Believe = true to oneself
FIRST TWO MINUTES	• Encourage understanding • Equality	• Nonverbal cues tell the (performance) story • Like content, translates in performance • Courage through uncertain moments

Figure 6.2. Beliefs & Identity—draft interview results (PM).

YOUR TURN, GIVE IT A TRY!

Using your own model, repeat this series of steps for each of the ten elements of the PM and TATE model. If your model isn't at this stage of readiness yet, use the idea of building a wooden chair or baking a three-layer themed birthday cake.

Once all ten elements are completed, the first draft (Table 6) should be easy to produce. Basically, this entails a step-by-step model of micro-moments that, together, produce the desired results. For "the first two minutes in a public speaking engagement," the draft needs to focus on two micro-moments in particular:

1. The few seconds immediately before beginning
2. The 120 seconds from the start of delivery. (The micro-moment immediately prior to starting delivery emerged as critical, explaining why it deserves separate consideration.)

TABLE 6. DRAFT INTERVIEW RESULTS IN TABULAR FORM—TATE & PM

	Commonalities		Differences That Make a Difference	
	Visible	**Hidden**	**Visible**	**Hidden**
Last few seconds before starting	Check technology, both visual and audio Wear attire appropriate to event and venue	Material is well understood and adequately rehearsed Openers are prepared and ready Some degree of confidence is present	Presenter visibly relaxed, talking or engaging in humorous banter Presenter quietly reflecting Material tailored to presenter's personal style	Presenter using positive self-talk, mind clear, focused, and ready for showtime Pre-presentation nerves starting to be harnessed (for energy) Visualization of the presentation done perfectly

continued

	Visible	Hidden	Visible	Hidden
First 120 seconds from the start of delivery	Presenter is making eye contact with attendees throughout the audience Voice speed and tonal variation are being monitored and moderated Body language is well-judged (hand, arm, or stage space movements) and appropriate Delivery is crisp and audible Nervous habits are not visible (e.g., rattling coins, or ums and ahs)	Initial presentation nerves are being managed Audience cues are being periodically evaluated and acted upon (e.g., moderated behavior, use of gestures, etc.) Transient moments of self-doubt are recognized and are being quietly worked through	Voice possesses good speed, variation, and tone throughout the presentation Presenter is actively exhibiting open and approachable nonverbal cues (e.g., smiling, open posture, easy manner) Presenter is varying delivery style based on real-time audience cues in order to build rapport with the audience	Presenter is adroitly reading and adapting effortlessly to audience cues (nonverbal in this 2-minute micro-moment) Initial presentation nerves (adrenaline) are being positively deployed as energy to "be on fire" in the moment Presenter is being true to authentic self Mind is systematically pacing through the process steps Presenter is experiencing positive alignment of self-image and experience

A fishbone diagram[10] (Figure 6.3) is a useful tool to visually reinforce these concepts.

---

10   Kaoru Ishikawa, 1968.

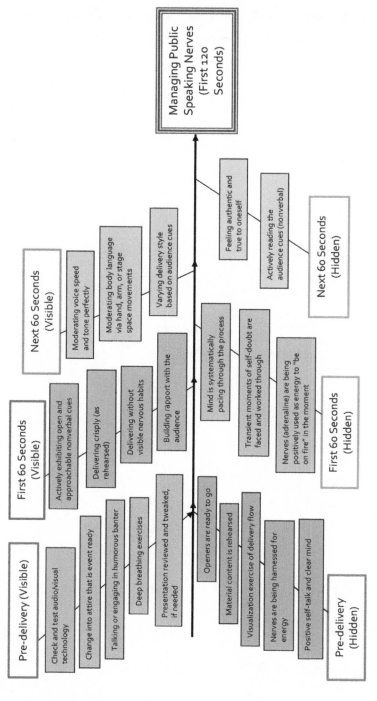

Figure 6.3. Draft interview results skill model—TATE and PM.

The next step is to validate the process model with each expert to confirm its accuracy and completeness.

Chapter 7

Closing the Gaps

C losing the gaps between the first draft and the final version of the skill model involves road-testing the draft model, and learning how to identify and eliminate or reduce differences identified. There are two ways to do this:

1. Observe the expert in action performing the skill concerned.
2. Perform a walk-through of the draft process model with each expert.

Observation is typically the best method; this is because you not only see the perfect model in action, but also there's no filter (other than any inherent observational bias). Using your draft process model as a reference, note any actions and behaviors from the live observation not already captured in your first draft. Also, be alert to any items in the draft that don't occur or do not appear required in practice. If observation is neither possible nor practical, the next-best approach is to walk through the model with the expert.

Ideally, assist the expert in choosing a moment in time other than their original moment (i.e., the moment used in creating the draft) so that the association can be viewed with a fresh perspective. (The process of working with an expert to choose a moment in time was covered in Chapter 5.)

The walk-through will undoubtedly identify at least a few differences. Simply note these, at this stage. Allow the expert to chat through their end-to-end experience, saving your exploratory questions until the end, while remembering to make notes you can review later. Once the associated walk-through is complete, query any differences noted.

Why do these differences occur at all? An activity, by its nature, contains two elements: what you can see and what you can't. Both elements need to be identified and contextualized in order to effectively replicate the process. As Charles Dickens wrote in *Hard Times*, "Now, what I want is Facts." The facts are what we're seeking here, so it is important to identify those observed activities that are unique to the expert concerned, and thus not generalizable. Additionally, any activity is generally linked to both beliefs and purposes. The process model must get to the heart of this in order to be effective. With any missing elements (differences) between the first draft and your observation now identified and noted, a debrief with the expert is needed.

Using, once again, the "first two minutes in a public speaking engagement" to illustrate nuances that typically emerge, we observe the following:

- Grouping data into themes increases the relevance of information. This is because it facilitates an analysis of the concepts behind the actions. For example, engaging in humorous banter, casual chit-chat, or deep-breathing exercises as "pre-delivery activities (visible)" are all different ways of "getting in the zone."
- Some activities require assumptions in order to produce meaningful teachable moments. For example, moderating body movements (such as hand movements) as a behavior to replicate

is only possible when the hands are actually free! This would fall under "venue logistics preparation," including access to your preferred audio solution (hands-free in our example). Imagine the onstage stress (possibly humor, depending on one's point of view) that could arise if gesticulating when physically confined by audio equipment!

- Rapport with the audience can be dissected during observation and a post-delivery debriefing.
- Clean (or clear) language refers to language freed from the all-too-common "um," "you know," "like," "uh," and all the other meaningless, sometimes annoying and repetitive fillers that can mar a live event. (You probably won't be surprised to learn that such language patterns aren't easily captured through memory associa-tions, not because the expert is unaware of them but because pride or self-protection cause them to be omitted from the discussion.)

With the observed differences noted and explored, the final model beckons!

Chapter 8

Developing a Final Model

With gaps identified and dealt with, the final model is ready for development. The easiest starting point in this phase is to update and extend the process flow diagram, using the additional insights gained from the live walk-through (or second interview). To illustrate, we'll stick with our "first two minutes in a public speaking engagement" example, which produced the updated process flow shown in Figure 8.1.

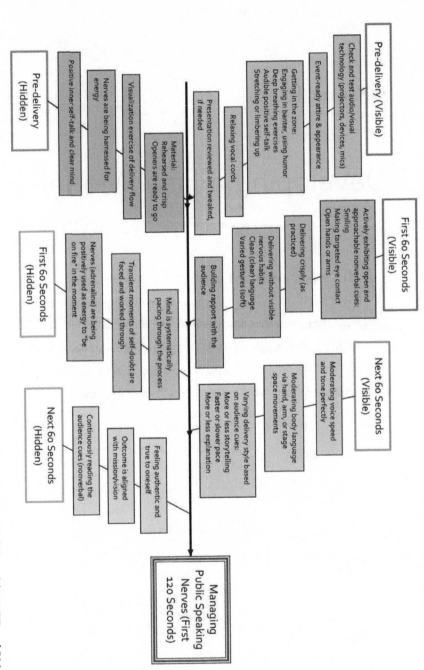

Figure 8.1. Updated and pretested skill model—TATE and PM.

Each of these boxes is, in itself, a teachable moment. Let's take one teachable moment: "Making targeted eye contact" from the "First 60 seconds (visible)" phase in the category of "Actively exhibiting open and approachable nonverbal cues."

This activity has its own micro-moments. For instance, speaker micro-moments could be:

1. Choosing three to six engaged and friendly faces throughout the audience
2. Making eye contact with each of the chosen individuals in turn, smiling using soft eyes (in other words: connect softly, meaning a friendly, open, unpressured connection)
3. Varying eye movement randomly between the selected individuals throughout the presentation—not obtrusively, but occasionally, at a pace that feels genuine and uncontrived

The result? An audience that feels engaged and involved, both in the presentation and in the speaker. Which is exactly what we're after!

Using a second teachable moment example: "Visualization exercise of delivery flow," located within the "Pre-delivery (hidden)" phase. Micro-moments here could include:

1. Finding a quiet, comfortable place.
2. Mentally running through opening line(s). Being able to mentally see, hear, and feel the warmly positive audience reaction. "(Everything can be used to make the visualization more potent: Include your own attire and the venue, if you're familiar with it.)"
3. Feeling the energy from the audience as they react to the presentation.

4. Visualizing tone moderation, speed of speech, and body movements. Seeing, sensing, and feeling the audience reaction to the
   energy buildup.

5. Absorbing positive energy from the applause at the end, the con-
   gratulatory handshakes, the vote of thanks, etc.

The result of this moment? It helps to get you in a positive, pumped-up,
and excited-to-perform mood!

These reflective teachable moment steps serve three purposes:

- To identify any residual skill steps that may not have surfaced
  beforehand during the expert interviews or walk-throughs.
- To reach "in the moment" skill readiness. The more practiced, the
  more effective it will prove in practice.
- To start shifting focus toward cementing a quiet confidence, the
  kind of confidence that draws the desired skill outcome to you
  and keeps it there.

Extending the public speaking process diagram to include these
additional micro-moments not only adds depth to the model but also
highlights further activities that might be useful. Using an extended form
of the same example ("First two minutes in a public speaking engagement"), Figure 8.2 depicts how adding a few micro-moments yields a
richer model.

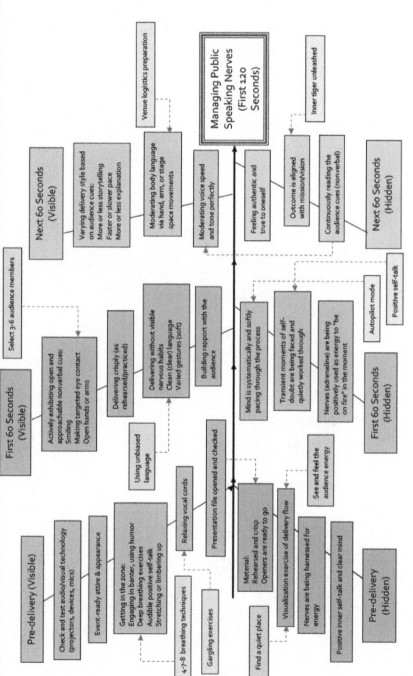

Figure 8.2. Final tested skill model—TATE and PM.

Returning to our lighthearted example of "Making the perfect omelet," we see a similar final model (Figure 8.3).

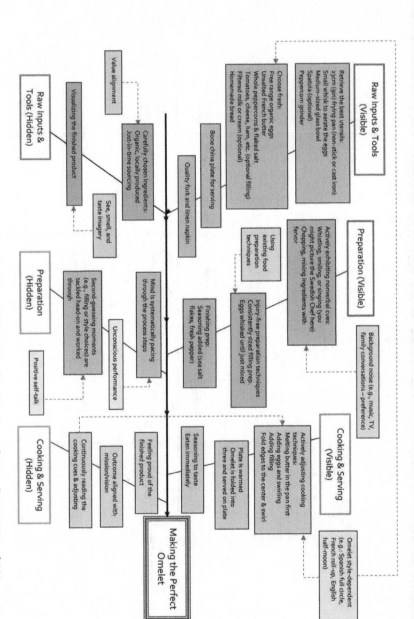

Figure 8.3. Final tested skill model of making the perfect omelet—TATE and PM.

Of course, your model for your chosen skill will be more intricate once you capture all the micro-moment activities, behaviors, and beliefs. (A link to the complete version of the "First two minutes of public speaking engagement" model is provided in the Appendix if you want to dive into that example a little further.)

With your final model complete, the next step is sharing the findings with each of your experts.

SHARING THE FINDINGS WITH YOUR EXPERTS

As we touched on in the initial meeting with our expert (Chapter 4), the final step in the modeling process is to share the process diagram (or the instruction manual, if you've opted for a narrative approach rather than a visual one) with each of the individuals who've shared their time and energy with you. One reason for this step is the recognition that the sum of us all is far greater than any individual. This is sometimes called the power of the "hive mind." Or as Blanchard succinctly put it, "None of us is as smart as all of us."

Another reason for sharing is that experts, like top-class athletes, also continually strive to improve their craft. (That's why top-class athletes *become* top-class!) The model here is designed to offer even long-established experts new insights into learning and development. In my experience, everyone participating gets at least one useful and relevant takeaway.

When I first began to share my public speaking mastery model, I was gratified to observe how even the starriest experts took something positive from the experience, which they embedded into their own processes (way of doing their "thing"). It was also a privilege to see firsthand how relatively small tweaks can lead to meaningful changes in experts and in experts-in-training alike. Here are just a few examples:

1. Improved delivery by using more engaging stories (better sharing)
2. Greater self-confidence thanks to positive self-talk
3. Faster rapport development due to additional interpersonal skill techniques
4. Improved ability to bring others along on the journey by employing punchier language

"Hmm," you think, "sounds a bit too easy." Actually, when modeling is done correctly, the benefits can be both swift and tangible. It's the *practical* application of modeling that is so powerful—what you relate to and truly understand, you can do!

Now you hold the keys. You have the know-how needed in order to replicate any skill. So let's take the next step in your adventure of endless possibilities and explore how to more quickly put it into practice in your own life!

Part Two

Implementation: Putting the Pedal to the Metal

You may be asking yourself: Where do I go from here? Well, exciting times lie just ahead! You are ready to apply this skill-replication model to perfect a skill in your own toolbox. Or possibly you're considering how to use the model to help others build a skill. Either way, you've already demonstrated commitment to change. Now you need to decide how best to transition the expert knowledge you have gleaned into skill mastery within you. You will take that information, define your dream, leverage your change preferences, and then put in the effort to execute.

In this section, we will cover the most common concerns:

- What obstacles might I run into as I perfect my desired skill?
- How will I know if the challenges I run into are typical or unique?

- What do I do if I plateau?
- How will I know if I'm hitting my mark?
- What will indicate that I have reached expertise?
- What should I do once I am an expert?

The answers to these questions and more will be revealed in the following pages.

In this part of the book, you'll learn how to—

1. Leverage your motivation and change styles, igniting a fire for self-change
2. Establish and execute a winning game plan
3. Surround yourself with the best support system
4. Enjoy success and help others do the same

This section will equip you with seven tools and techniques needed to take everything you learned from your expert, convert it into an achievable process, and master your desired skill.

We begin by taking a little time to better understand individual motivators and change preferences, which will help you determine *your* best way forward. Structure goals to ignite your passion; goals miss the mark when plagued by indifference or dispassion.

Chapter 9

Understanding Motivators and Change Styles

When undertaking any change, humans display a predictable pattern of response. That pattern is a product of our view of the world as described in the Introduction. We will look at two aspects in particular: motivation and change style. Understanding these two aspects of yourself is critical to create fully achievable milestones that are much less likely to be abandoned.

MOTIVATORS

As briefly introduced in Chapter 5, motivation moves in two basic directions: toward something (seekers) or away from something (avoiders). As you may guess, a toward motivation is a positive frame, whereas an away-from motivation is a negative (or avoidance) frame.

Example

Goal: I want to lose ten pounds.

Toward—I will make healthy food choices to achieve a healthy weight.

Away from—To help manage my weight downwards, I won't eat any junk food.

The simple difference is that an away-from motivation tends to include words like don't, won't, can't, or never. Toward motivation tends to include words like will, do, always, or want.

Interestingly, you can add an away-from motivation within a toward goal to emphasize why the toward aspect of the change goal is the best option. For instance—

Goal: Encourage my spouse to eat healthily (perhaps not a great idea in real life, but useful here)

Toward—You will enjoy having a healthy and beach-ready body.

Away from—Healthy eating habits will help avoid a trip to the doctor.

An away-from motivator is most effective when it relates to a need (or value) that matters to you, such as a need for financial security or personal well-being.

Goal: To be a sought-after, charismatic, and inspiring public speaker helping others elevate themselves, thereby avoiding any period of unemployment.

In this case, the toward motivator is the *charismatic and inspiring public speaker helping others.* The away-from motivator is *avoiding any period of unemployment.*

By listening to patterns of speech, you can pick up on preferred language. In their everyday communication, avoiders tend to use away-from, and seekers tend to use toward phraseology. The key in our context is using this to align milestone objectives with the individual's natural preference (otherwise it may serve as a de-motivator).

For individuals who are naturally motivated by the away-from style, an alternative technique seeks to amplify avoidance consequences through a three-step process (Table 7). These three steps clarify what is to be avoided by reflecting on the impact of switching your approach, the impact relative to your life timeline, and actively considering alternatives. (In this instance, remember to use the 4Rs from Chapter 4 [Figure 4.4] on yourself throughout, particularly Respect and Recognition.)

TABLE 7. THREE-STEP ALTERNATIVE MOTIVATOR APPROACH

Process Step	Reflective Questions to Ask Yourself
1. Assess the impact of switching to a toward approach.	What will I miss out on if I don't do anything? What happens if I continue to do things as I do and do not take steps to change? How will my friends (colleagues) see me if I don't take the steps to change? How will my loved ones view me if I don't take the steps to change? How will I feel if I take the steps to change?
2. Assess the impact relative to a snapshot of your life timeline. *Looking into your past:* This step is designed to help an individual see (in a dispassionate way) the impact not acting so far has had. It is about objectively recognizing the impact of past decisions on the present. *Looking into your future:* This step is designed to help an individual visualize the effects of not taking action moving forward. The projection could be mere months or could be years, dependent on the magnitude of the change that will be undertaken (for example, achieving a healthy weight might take a few months, whereas perfecting Mandarin may take a few years).	How does it feel to see yourself in the future if you don't undertake the change? What have you lost out on by not making the changes? How do others view you after you haven't taken on the change? How does it feel now, recognizing that changes that could or should have happened in the past didn't? What have you lost out on by not taking action so far?

continued

3. Consider the alternatives. The focus shifts here to what happens if you *do* act now.	What benefits will taking action now give you? What will happen once those benefits are achieved? How will the change benefit your loved ones, friends, and colleagues? What other beneficial outcomes can you foresee?

It is important to remind yourself of the consequences of not making your change now. Once this is clear in your mind and you can see no reasonable alternative but to be committed, the motivation to perfect your desired skill is where it needs to be. Let's return to our public speaking example:

Goal: To be a sought-after, charismatic, and inspiring public speaker helping others elevate themselves.

This centers on a toward motivational style, though the goal objective could be augmented by including the double motivation approach (incorporating both toward and away-from motivators).

Double Motivation Goal: To be a sought-after, charismatic, and inspiring public speaker helping others elevate themselves, thereby achieving thought-leader recognition and avoiding the industry-prevalent risk of obscurity and subsequent financial hardship.

CHANGE STYLES

Let me explain why understanding your preferred style is helpful in this journey. Learning is simply an exercise in self-initiated change. There is a continuum of change preference styles, from individuals favoring an incremental change approach through those preferring a pragmatic approach to those who thrive on disruptive change approaches (Figure 9.1).

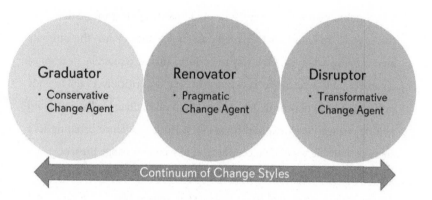

Figure 9.1. Change style range.

Graduator

This style lends itself well to problem identification, knowing who can provide helpful information, and to integrating moving parts to achieve a defined outcome. Significant change challenges for this style include an occasional, exaggerated focus on rules and stubborn resistance to input from others. Conservative change styles tend to thrive in the details, often at the expense of the big picture. In our context, this means a graduator benefits by remaining consciously aware of change impact (on him or herself and those around them), asking others for feedback or input, and keeping one eye on the ultimate prize throughout.

Example

Goal: To be a sought-after, charismatic, and inspiring public speaker helping others elevate themselves.

In public speaking, a graduator could easily get lost in the details of the speech. To counteract this risk, assess whether or not the ultimate goal is being achieved. One way to confirm this is to practice in front of a camera. Self-assessment is a powerful way to critically evaluate your performance. Replay provides objective and immediate feedback. Would you be engaged and inspired if you were in the audience listening to a speaker with the tone of voice, physical movements, stage presence, and content that you are seeing in the replay? Is your presentation style charismatic and inspirational in its delivery? Is your content structured and delivered in a manner that elevates the audience? If not, why not?

Renovator

This type tends to address issues as they occur, take a realistic and practical approach to change, and ask others for their input. Significant challenges for this change style are the risk of paralysis (being unable to make a decision or stuck in uncertainty), not making timely decisions, or taking timely action and trying to please everyone. Pragmatic change styles tend to thrive on keeping an open mind and trying different things to achieve the desired outcome. In our context, this means that a renovator benefits by being more decisive (even in the face of imperfect information), keeping a closer eye on due dates, and using peripheral awareness (instead of concentrated focus) of their impact on others.

Example

Goal: To be a sought-after, charismatic, and inspiring public speaker helping others elevate themselves.

In public speaking, a renovator could easily fall behind while trying to decide which speech content to include and which to exclude. A counteraction to this risk is to regularly check progress against due dates leading up to the event to determine whether or not the ultimate goal will be achieved. For a renovator, peer assessments are a powerful way to critically evaluate performance. There are several ways to objectively confirm your status: How is your presentation content going to meet audience expectations for a charismatic, inspirational, and elevating delivery? Have you tested delivery with individuals you trust to be honest with you? If not, why not? Are they engaged and inspired listening to your presentation, considering your communication style (e.g., tone, speed, variation of voice, and presence) and content?

Disruptor

This style tends to challenge the status quo, develops a risk-based contingency plan, focuses on the big picture, and always looks forward to the future. Significant challenges include a risk of losing focus and chasing the next shiny thing, making impulsive decisions, or developing a plan that doesn't adequately consider the environment within which it will happen. Transformative change styles tend to thrive on seeing possibilities (which others often do not yet see) and almost obsessively drive to make it a reality, thereby achieving the end goal. In our context, this means that a disruptor benefits by sleeping on an idea/goal to disrupt impulsive decision making, using a disciplined goal-setting methodology to mitigate the risk of overlooking something, and actively seeking feedback from conservator types during plan development.

Example:

Goal: To be a sought-after, charismatic, and inspiring public speaker helping others elevate themselves.

In public speaking, a disruptor style could easily try to boil the ocean by obsessing on shiny new technology devices or software (before they're tried and tested), developing content without adequately validating audience expectations, or losing focus by thinking about other project possibilities. Counteractions to these risks could include establishing (or outsourcing) new technology testing periods during downtime, using a structured speaking engagement template to consistently assess all relevant aspects of the engagement expectations, and establishing motivational reminders to remain engaged with the project. For a disruptor, peer assessments are also a helpful way to evaluate whether the delivery is on point in meeting its objectives. How is your planned speaking delivery (e.g., content, technology, and style) going to meet attendee expectations? Have you tested the speech delivery with a small representative group of individuals for their reaction? Did any delivery hiccups surface? How did the test group rate your performance in meeting the objectives of charismatic, inspiring, and elevating?

Each of the three change styles brings strengths as well as potential blind spots. Understanding your preferred style enables you to actively consider areas for improvement. This ability to avoid pitfalls secures higher-quality outcomes, a giant leap toward mastering the skill.

Awareness of one's style and the attributes that tend to be found in the style helps you immensely in mastering your chosen skill, as we will discuss in the next two chapters. We will also get into what to do if you fall short of the goal in Chapter 14.

YOUR TURN, GIVE IT A TRY!

Take some time to determine your own motivator and change style preference. Identify the natural risks that may lurk beneath the surface as a result of these preferences. Make a note of your potential blind spots; these will help you in the next section.

Knowing a little more about yourself, you're ready to move on to the technique to clearly identify the target or skill level you're aiming for. It begins with daydreaming, a wonderful childhood skill that is sometimes lost in adulthood. Beginning with the end in mind facilitates your journey toward excellence.

Chapter 10

A Moment to Dream

Some individuals embarking on a journey of change do so without a clear view of the destination in mind. Now, that might be a great strategy for a spontaneous vacation with your partner, but it is generally ineffective for self-improvement. Why? Without clarity of purpose and definition of success, how will you know you've reached your destination?

A powerful technique, coined the Disney Creative Strategy,[11] helps us clarify what we are aiming for. Used by Walt Disney himself, this two-stage coaching technique is employed around the world to help an individual achieve something they want: a skill, a career change, or a life change. There are two phases: preparatory and execution.

Let's start with an explanation and then a couple of examples.

PREPARATORY PHASE

Step 1: Dream big!

Settle for nothing less than a stretch objective. Let nothing hold you back from something you'd like to achieve; a change you'd like to make in your

---

11 Robert Dilts, 1994.

life, work, or profession; or a personal change such as improving your fitness or health. The technique is wasted on anything less than something that will push you to really develop over time.

Step 2: Choose three physical locations

Select three physical locations (inside or outside). Ideally the locations should have characteristics that match the state of mind required for the activity and are located reasonably close to one another so you don't lose momentum between activities. Your location choices should consider four attributes.

- Dream: conducive to a creative and open frame of mind. I prefer a quiet, open, and comfortable space, ideally a favorite Adirondack chair.

- Plan: conducive to structure, process, and methodology. I favor a table (and chair) on the deck to make notes or create diagrams.

- Critique: conducive to analysis, assessment, and diagnosing. I tend to choose a backyard bench under a tree where I can escape into my thoughts and stress-test the plan.

- Neutral: conducive to clearing the mind and resetting thinking. I tend to walk into the house for a complete change of scenery.

1. **Dream:** Allow your imagination to run free in this location. Imagine all of the benefits that emerge from your dream becoming reality. See it, feel it, hear it all occurring.

2. **Plan:** In this location, your plan is entirely achievable. Focus on all the steps needed to make it reality.

3. **Critique:** In this space, actively poke holes in the plan to identify gaps or problems. Only focus on the plan—not the dream—and identify weaknesses, threats, and potential problems to ensure the plan's success. Remember to leave resolution of any issues you identify in this role to the planning role.

4. **Neutral (optional):** Add a fourth neutral location, from which to momentarily step out of the technique if you want to.

Step 3: Associate on-fire feelings to each role

Here, you simply want to recall moments of personal success for each role and re-experience them in your chosen physical locations. This will help you in the execution phase.

1. **Dream:** Recall positive experiences when you were fantasizing, daydreaming, or strategizing a life goal and vividly relive a couple of those episodes in the dream location.

2. **Plan:** Now remember good times where you successfully planned a project at work, a once-in-a-lifetime vacation, or a home renovation, and then step into those on-fire moments in your chosen plan location.

3. **Critique:** Think about a couple of successful instances where you constructively critiqued the plan of a colleague or one of your own plans and relive those winning experiences in your critique location.

EXECUTION PHASE

You're now ready to submit your own "dream" to this technique.

Let's look at public speaking to show the technique in action. The dream is to be a sought-after, charismatic, and inspiring public speaker helping others elevate themselves.

Step 1: Dream

Physically step into your chosen location to dream and connect with the feelings from your on-fire dreaming-freely moments. Now bring the big picture of your desired skill, "a highly sought-after, charismatic, and inspiring speaker," into your dream space. See yourself living it vividly and without limitations, using an anything-is-possible attitude.

Example

In the public-speaking moment, I want to be charismatic and inspiring to help others elevate themselves. The moments are playing out in a plenary holding hundreds of people. It is 9 a.m., time for the sixty-minute keynote address. I am wearing a white shirt and blue jeans, and I'm surrounded by my sound, lighting, and video crew (they travel throughout the year with me). I know if I nail this event, I will positively influence the lives of the attendees and equip them with an energized and renewed sense of purpose. I will know that I hit my mark through audience engagement in the moment and, later, through post-event feedback and new client opportunities.

Questions to facilitate your own exploration:
These questions are most effective when spoken out loud and answered in the same way for each of the roles.

- What do I want to achieve?

- What are the benefits of achieving this dream?
- When and where will it begin?
- What will I be doing, and who will I be doing it with?
- What will achieving it mean to me and to those close to me?
- How will I know when I have achieved it?

Step 2: Plan

With the dream clearly in mind, physically step into the plan location and connect to your on-fire planning moments. Believing that your dream is fully realizable, define the plan that will make it happen.

Example

In the public-speaking moment, I need to be in a positive frame of mind associated with my on-fire, best-self anchor. To do this, I must prepare for the event by knowing my audience, my material, and the technology being used, and I need to be skilled in managing my state of mind, projecting confidence, communicating with clarity, understanding the topic, and being prepared for any question. Some of the steps required include asking about the venue attendees, the organizer's objectives, the technology in place, and the venue facilities available. These steps are important, as they clarify elements that influence the speech content, delivery options, format chosen, attire worn, additional technology needs, and my crew needs. To make the objective a reality, I will need four crew members (working ten hours to prepare and two hours on event day), customized online post-event resources (two hours to adapt existing resources), and preparation time (two hours with the event organizers and four hours of event prep time). I will know that I hit my mark when my pre-event checks occur without a glitch and later, through post-event feedback.

Questions to facilitate your own exploration:
This step is most effective with a practical and realistic mindset. Strive for a manageable plan that is sufficiently detailed and clear.

- What do I need to do in order to achieve the dream?
- What are the milestone steps or phases of my dream? How are they sequenced?
- What baby steps are needed to achieve each milestone?
- Why is this step necessary? And this one? And this one?
- What is needed to make it happen in terms of people, time, and money (or other resources)?
- How will I know when I have achieved each milestone?

Step 3: Critique

With a plan in mind (or written or digitally captured, if you prefer, from Step 2), step into the critique location and connect with your on-fire moment here.

Example

The public-speaking event is vulnerable to unplanned technology failures (screens, laptops, electronic whiteboards, etc.), illness of critical path team members, the presenter's health, and unforeseen traffic issues (such as unplanned road closures or traffic accidents). A gap in the plan is the lack of resource availability relative to other events being run (which also need crew members) and the lack of contingency planning or fallback if a vulnerability occurs on the day (or shortly before). The plan affects the crew members, the presenter (me), the organizer's team, and all attendees. The plan derail risks are associated primarily with unplanned and noncontrollable events. Controllable items all include a standard working backup strategy (including in the event the speaker is taken ill). There are no other areas of immediate concern in the plan.

Questions to facilitate your own exploration:
This step is most effective with a constructive but critical mindset. Strive to poke holes in your plan (but don't try to solve them).

- What are the threats and weaknesses in my plan?
- What are the gaps in the plan steps?
- Is there anything that doesn't make sense in the plan or may create unintended consequences?
- Who will be affected by the plan (favorably and unfavorably)?
- What might derail the plan in terms of people, places, or resources?
- Are there any other areas of concern in my plan?

We've completed the first pass of the plan, but we're not done yet. Big ideas and dreams understandably need a number of passes between the planning and critiquing phases of the process. Vulnerabilities and gaps identified in the critique stage are returned to the planning location for resolution.

EXECUTING MORE PASSES OF THE PLAN

Pace the plan by moving back and forth between the planning and critiquing stages until all significant weaknesses, vulnerabilities, and gaps are resolved (see Figure 10.1). For ambitious dreams, you may have to run through the plan a few times a week, until it is second nature.

Hint: Only change your dream if you're sure that a workable plan is genuinely unachievable (or unachieved).

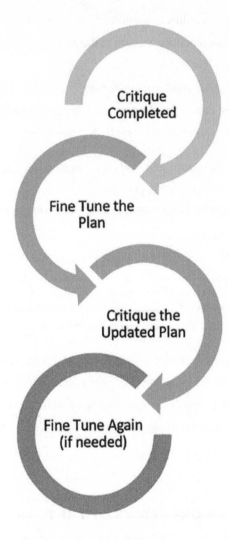

Figure 10.1. Pacing the plan.

Let's bring it all together with another example to highlight how the dream might look and feel on an integrated basis. I like to find a quiet space where I can escape into my head for a while. You might prefer more ambient noise or somewhere busy; it is a personal choice.

I step into my dream and imagine that I'm thinking about how to improve my happiness and quality of life—infinitely big outcomes (remember, this technique is best for ambitious ideas)! I start by vividly visualizing the dream:

- A getaway waterfront property that is minimally 250 meters from the nearest neighbor and takes me no more than four hours to reach from home, door to door. It is a stone property with low-maintenance land, minimally 60 percent sunshine hours per year, within twenty minutes of amenities, and with a sustainable cost of living.

- The property interior is stone and plaster, full of character, has a central fireplace, a million-dollar lake view through floor-to-ceiling windows, evening sunsets into the family room, and lots of space for the kids and our two dogs to safely play.

- The property has many modern conveniences, including lightning-fast Internet, satellite TV, and an office space overlooking the lake.

- Having a secret getaway will allow me to escape the pressures of my career, recharge my batteries, and spend quality time with my loved ones and friends.

- The target timeline is within one year from now, with debt of no more than $1 million.

- This dream creates feelings of peace, contentment, and connection with my partner and joy with my children.

I can imagine this property; I can see our family living in it and enjoying life moments. It feels right. Now I want the dream!

This clarity spurs me to create a plan to convert it into reality, when I will physically step into this space. In this phase, I need to consider the detail necessary to make it all happen. In this phase, the plan materializes:

- A budget is set: the maximum purchase price is $2 million, consisting of a $1 million cash deposit and a $1 million mortgage. The budget will be lender preapproved before any purchase offer is made in order to avoid financing conditions.

- An area of search is established, around Grand Lake, Colorado.

- My partner will perform the initial search to narrow our property viewings to six suitable options within our budget. The search may be land only or an established property. A land-only purchase will be capped at $1.2 million, allowing for $800,000 to build a home and landscape the property.

- The house search will start on February 1, 202x.

- We will achieve success when we've purchased a property that achieves our must-haves, within our budget and our timeline.

The picture and plan are crystallizing; now I need to stress-test it in the critique phase. Here, I'm looking for holes and gaps. There is no attempt to solve them in this phase, just identification:

- The plan depends on property availability, something over which there is limited control.

- It also depends on my partner's time. She's tied up with consulting projects for the next ninety days so one-quarter of the first year is gone.

- The deposit cash value depends on an investment portfolio growing at 1.5 percent per quarter. The market outlook is mixed, so it is a risk.

- Purchasing an existing property requires a renovation budget, which could range up to $200,000, depending on the condition of the house.

The gaps and risks become more apparent, so now the process goes back into planning to address them. I physically step into the planning space again.

- The timeline is extended to fifteen months; the quarter lost with my partner's consulting projects cannot be mitigated in a workable way for us.

- The portfolio can be sufficiently diversified to mitigate downside risk using some financial instrument vehicles.

This iterative process goes back and forth until the plan is as solid as a rock and will enable you to achieve your dream, one you can see, feel, hear, and experience realistically in your mind now! You get the idea.

YOUR TURN, GIVE IT A TRY!

Take your own stretch objective and pace it through the model. If you don't have one yet, practice using the dream of playing the piano like Angela Hewitt or playing soccer like Pelé or Lionel Messi.

Now that you have a clear understanding of the outcome you seek and a high-level workable plan to achieve it, we can move into developing a more detailed understanding of what's next, then next, and so forth. From this point forward, it is all about your needs and aligning the fully achievable plan with milestones and checkpoints. The next natural step is establishing a plan that sets out fully achievable objectives with clear milestones, deliverables, and timelines and incorporates new habits and meaningful feedback loops.

Chapter 11

Setting Relevant Milestones

With your high-level plan in hand, it is time to translate the dream into bite-size pieces. Mastering a skill needs a model that goes beyond setting goals. Why? Goals are framed around a conscious process leading to a destination and, therefore, are too constrained for skill development. This journey seeks an outcome: It is about mobilizing. If my outcome is a strong and happy relationship with my spouse, I am unlikely to reach this as a "goal"; however, as an outcome, it unconsciously structures my daily interaction choices, communication style, and behaviors with my spouse. This is the power we are seeking in our approach to setting our skill-perfecting milestones.

An example clarifies the difference between goals and outcomes:

Goal	Outcome
Prepare a romantic, child-free dinner for my partner and serve it on the backyard deck on July 13 at 7 p.m.	I want to be a loving, trustworthy, respectful husband, using open communication daily with my wife (or, insert your preferred terms).

We have all heard of the traditional SMART[12] goal method, which most of us find tedious or ineffective in practice, even with perfectly defined objectives. Under this method, it is easy to end up with goals that look impressive on a sheet of paper, but that is also where they usually end up staying!

Modeling behavior is all about how you influence an outcome that has not yet materialized. It is this step above simple goal setting and attainment that we are aiming for and where the power of Neuro-linguistic Programming is invaluable, as illustrated throughout Part One. The tool in question is the Well-Formed Outcomes[13] technique, which has been further improved into the PECSAW[14] model. These two models define outcomes that focus and build on positive aspects, tapping directly into motivators and setting them apart from traditional goal-setting models.

Outcomes are helpful when plotting your big idea into a journey that is actionable, meaningful, and achievable. Your idea goes from something big and fuzzy to something tangible and motivational (toward), and where you move from being a passenger to a driver. Outcomes become self-achievable. The PECSAW model builds in the following aspects:

Positive

Evidence

Context

Self-achievable

Advantages and Disadvantages

Worthwhile

The PECSAW model adds two elements to the Well-Formed Outcomes model:

---

12 George T. Doran, 1981.

13 Bandler & Grinder, 1979.

14 Reg Connolly, Pegasus NLP, 1998.

- Advantages and Disadvantages: Objectives need to consider the wider environment.
- Worthiness: An explicit element that connects goal setting to wider strategic objectives or outcomes to ensure alignment.

With your high-level dream plan from Chapter 10 in hand, you can now convert identified steps into an outcome using the following six-step PECSAW framework.

Positive is about focusing on what you *do* want (framing something in the positive pushes/pulls thinking away from a problem, excuse, or rationalizing mindset). It is the first step in embedding a belief in the goal or objective.

The questions to consider in this aspect:

- What do you want?
- What else do you want?

Example (recalling the first two minutes of public speaking)

What do I want?

"I want to feel confidence as I walk toward the platform using 'stage-nerves' as positive energy from which to launch into my talk."

"I want my voice to project confidence and credibility from the moment I start speaking."

Evidence means defining up front the criteria by which you will recognize achievement of the goal or outcome.

The questions to think about:

- What will you see (build a vivid storyboard to get a clear picture)?
- What will others see?

- How exactly will you know?
- What will you hear that tells you the goal has been achieved?

Example

What will I or others see?

"I will see audience members engaging with me via smiles, attentive body language, and head nodding."

What will I hear?

"I will hear laugher, impromptu applause, verbal acknowledgment of what is heard, and spontaneous questions."

Context is knowing the conditions under which you want the outcome to be achieved.

Helpful questions here are:

- Where will this outcome be taking place?
- When will this skill be occurring?
- When do you not want it to be occurring?
- Who will be around when you are doing "your thing"?
- What do I want to achieve?

Example

What do I want to achieve?

"I want my keynote address on March 1 to appear effortless and inspire the audience to take control of their financial future and well-being," or

"I want to be confident taking and answering questions in the twenty-minute Q&A period following my presentation to the Medical Education, Health Sciences, and Patient Care conference attendees on September 14."

Self-achievable is accepting that outcomes (goals or objectives) must be within your circle of influence or control.

Questions to address:

- Is your goal self-dependent or dependent on others?
- How will I achieve these goals?
- Who else needs to be involved (or will be involved) to achieve the outcome?
- If you identify a dependence, how can you reframe it to become self-reliant?
- What support or resources do you need to be able to achieve your objective?
- What do you personally need to do?

Example

How will I achieve it?

"I will personally deliver the desired inspiring outcome with the support of my dedicated sound, lighting, and video crew using Acme Presentation Software. I will use the content I prepared specifically for the audience's needs."

Advantages and Disadvantages is the recognition that every choice (goal, objective, and outcome) has a trade-off decision, meaning that using resources in one area subtracts them for use in other areas.

Questions will focus on the pros and cons:

- Knowing what it takes to make the objective a reality, do you remain passionate about it?
- What motivates and inspires you to reach the goal?

- Is the expected outcome going to be aligned with the quadrants (family/friends, career, social, and spiritual) of your life?
- What benefits and downsides do you see if you deliver on the objective as intended?
- What will you have to forgo in order to deliver on this outcome?

Example

What are the benefits and downsides (if applicable)?

"I am passionate about achieving the outcome because it is an opportunity to positively influence 1,000 physicians during the course of the two-hour session to adopt a better way of treating diabetes, which will improve patients' quality of life. The downside is it will take me two weekends of preparation time for the session, which means I will miss my four-year-old daughter's ballet recital and my seven-year-old son's baseball game."

Worthwhile is the final motivational question to assess whether or not the payoff is worth the effort.

Questions that get to the heart of the matter:

- Is this outcome worth your time and effort?
- What benefits will it attract?
- Why is it important?
- How does it feel to know you are going to do it?
- What have you learned in planning the outcome that convinces you to do it?
- Are the advantages of doing it outweighing the disadvantages, or can I mitigate the disadvantages in some way, making the payoff worth it?

Example

Is it worth my time?

"Conservatively, the outcome will improve the lives of 50 percent of conference attendees' patients, or approximately 20,000 patients. Patients will on average live five years longer and experience 60 percent fewer complications throughout their lives. The societal benefit exceeds the cost: The one-time sacrifice of not attending my children's events and the forty hours it will take me to prepare and deliver on the two-hour conference event slot."

An integrated example

Let's demonstrate applying the PECSAW model using an element from Chapter 6: "Managing Public Speaking Nerves—First 120 Seconds" reproduced in Figure 11.1. (Hint: remember to leverage your motivator and change style preferences to your advantage when framing your outcomes.)

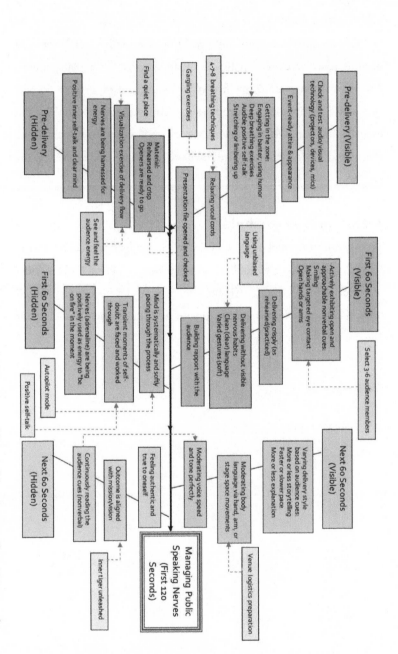

Figure 11.1. Managing public speaking nerves—first 120 seconds.

For simplicity, we'll narrow down the illustration, focusing on a branch of the outcome: Nerves (adrenaline) are being positively used as energy to "be on fire" in the moment.

Positive: List all positive aspects; your mind needs them embedded (this is the basis for the unconscious structuring):

"I want to feel confidence as I walk toward the platform using 'stage-nerves' as positive energy from which to launch. I want my self-talk to be positive and calming. I want my presentation material to reflect my communication style and the audience needs. I want my voice to be confident, clear, and articulate." *And so on . . .*

Evidence: Aim for a vivid picture of what is happening and how it links with the outcome—in this example, "being on fire"[15] in the moment. Add detail to your picture; it needs to be very clear in your mind what you are aiming for and what interconnected things need to occur for the outcome to materialize.

- Positive self-talk is occurring within me—I am actively using the 4Rs (Chapter 4).
- Physically energized in the moment—I am standing tall, walking with confident purpose.
- Mentally prepared—I am anchored to my "on-fire" resource, I am passionate about the purpose.
- Vocal cords are relaxed—pre-delivery vocal exercises completed; I'm hydrated.
- Ends in a standing ovation—my "on-fire" passion ignites enthusiasm and audience engagement.

---

15 "Being on fire" refers to a person who is very enthusiastic, excited, or passionate about something (Collins Dictionary).

Context: It is important to understand when you should and should not use the outcome, particularly when rapport is a key differentiator in success or failure!

Desirable moments to call upon for "being on fire":

- Speaking venues: These events benefit from triggering the association to being "on fire."
- Networking events: Business, association, or other networking moments also benefit.

Undesirable moments for "being on fire":

- Spousal interactions: Authenticity works best here for rapport; "being on fire" tends to break rapport within more intimate relationships by appearing overbearing.
- Serious conversations: Performance coaching or teaching life lessons need a softer rapport approach.

Self-achievable: The aim is always self-reliance; however, that is not always practical or productive for outcomes. Your aim is controlling as much as possible the required resource contributions (such as confirming a time commitment and location, clarifying expectations, etc.).

- Technique acquisition: By September 30, complete an NLP core skills program to acquire key techniques needed to master "being on fire" (4Rs, anchors, PECSAW, Panel of Experts, Personality Map, and more).
- Technique application: By December 31, practice the techniques in at least twenty varied situations; ask for recipient feedback on how it felt to them (e.g., genuine, contrived, clunky?).

- Record application: By November 15, digitally record the technique application, replay it and self-critique, improve.

Advantages and Disadvantages: Recognizing the benefits and the drawbacks is reinforcing, meaning your eyes are wide open, with growing clarity as to why it is a worthy pursuit for *you*.

- Advantages include the opportunity to inspire, ignite in others interest/passion in a topic, get your message across to others, managing pre-stage nerves, harness internal energies, and present with confidence.
- Disadvantages include the time and effort to complete the NLP core skills program (five days) and time to practice the technique applications.

Worthwhile: At this stage of the outcome process, if you are not convinced, then frankly you should not pursue the outcome (or you've skipped over the element responses and need to revisit those). This element either seals the deal, or is the proverbial nail in the coffin. Examples of worthwhile outcomes might be delineated as follows:

- Mastering "being on fire" is expected to result in a 62 percent increase in public speaking engagements.
- For each 10 percent step-increase in engagements delivered, $50,000 is added in net profit and four new permanent roles are created.
- Igniting just 5 percent of the audience as new passionate ambassadors of greener economies will result in a 9 percent reduction in greenhouse gases, save 3,500 lives through cleaner air and water, and create 200,000 new green jobs.

To sum it up, this outcome model helps enlighten a storyboard, image, or understanding of the journey from the outset. This results in an unconscious structure for all subsequent effort. The dream plan and subsequent drill-down using PECSAW with outcome branches results in milestones or mini outcomes toward the more ambitious dream (e.g., your desired mastered skill). These milestones or mini outcomes are self-assessable (or assessable with others), including against wider values and priorities such as business activities, family goals, or community events. The underlying theme throughout is to practice, practice, practice—in other words, it becomes a habit. It is this acquisition and embedding that ultimately leads to the desired outcome: mastery or perfection.

A final note: The model is also helpful in establishing or clarifying personal or career dreams, wishes, or any other desired stretch outcome. The possibilities are infinite!

YOUR TURN, GIVE IT A TRY!
Take your own high-level dream plan (and final model from your interviews) and work through PECSAW. If you don't have one yet, use one of the models from the book.

With your plan now defined, it's time to address the next questions: With so many moving parts in an outcome model, where do I start first? What should I prioritize and how do I make that decision? What if I can't do it all, then what? Are there any shortcut tricks that will accelerate the outcome?

Chapter 12

Prioritizing Your Focus

Whenever the outcome involves self-improvement or a significant life change, the decision is fundamentally about innovation. You are innovating yourself in some way: mastering a skill, changing careers, changing your mindset, raising healthy, well-adjusted children, or any number of personal changes.

Because this is the outcome *journey* I talk about, you will assess these changes very differently than you might do in assessing a particular goal. We will hold the thought of assessing success and come back to it in Chapter 14.

The concept I want to introduce before getting into priorities is the blueprint, a vivid picture or plan of who you want to become. It is a reflection of the next better version of yourself. Your moment to dream (Chapter 10) set the foundation for this picture. Now we introduce a deeper understanding of why and how a new, future you will reset your reticular activating system (RAS)—a fancy term for resetting your personal information-processing filters (refer back to the Introduction—our beliefs, attitudes, values, and nurtured conditions). Filters are essential—they protect us from information overload—but they can be problematic in some cases, particularly when information our filters deem irrelevant is subsequently lost or buried deep in our unconscious mind. We never see this information; it effectively never appears within our consciousness.

Let me illustrate the principle using a simple experience most of us have had: buying a car. Imagine that your showroom-new yellow convertible is ready to pick up. You sign the remaining paperwork, get your keys, and pull cautiously out of the lot lest you damage your new toy! As you drive home, amazingly, every fifth car you see is yellow. It is not that yellow cars have just appeared everywhere. It's simply that your filters previously "buried" the yellow cars in your unconscious mind as information the reticular activating system deemed irrelevant at the time. It happened so quickly that your conscious mind didn't register yellow cars before the filters instantaneously "buried" the images. You started noticing them when your filter was reset; yellow cars became relevant to you due to your purchase. The information was then relayed to your conscious mind, so in that sense they suddenly appear everywhere.

This filtering process applies to all areas of our lives, including money, love, success, and happiness. If we do not focus on these things, they too will be "buried" as the filters start deeming them irrelevant information. Effectively, they become unseen by you. Why does this matter with self-improvements? For every desired outcome in life, we need to set our filters so that the reticular activating system will funnel this now-relevant information to the conscious mind. The conscious mind in turn actively works on making it a reality. The best way to set the filters is through your outcomes. When you play in your head a vivid storyboard—images, pictures, or movies of your future self doing the skill—that does the resetting for you. The more vivid the storyboards are, the more effective the filters will be. This powerful, yet invisible, process is part of the secret to mastering any skill—it effortlessly does some of the heavy lifting for you!

By linking this visualization and filter reset technique with prioritizing our focus, outcomes start to feel less overwhelming than goals. Outcomes seem more achievable and within reach (and perhaps we already experience the outcome in some cases), whereas goals can seem out of reach, atop a mountain yet to be climbed.

In business, there are many ways to prioritize:

- Managing upward to make decision makers happy
- Scheduling goal deliveries by return on investment (ROI) to the organization
- Deciding delivery priorities by stakeholder or organizational value impacts (e.g., green outcomes before profit outcomes or employee welfare before shareholder priorities)
- Low-hanging fruit, otherwise known as quick wins, which typically prioritize time more than ROI or any other possible performance measure

All are valid ways of establishing priorities and are aligned to one or more company values. For instance, does the organization value profit over people or vice versa? Another important aspect of prioritization is identifying what is mission critical or a key dependency. For instance, a child must learn to stand before walking and walk before running. This critical pathway needs to be fleshed out to minimize outcome effort.

The same basic principles hold true for non-business outcomes. Recalling our example of "being on fire," a critical dependency for the outcome is completion of the NLP core program. This is because the capabilities necessary to achieve the "being on fire" outcome lie, in part, with having certain techniques and tools in our toolbox. This mini milestone is a critical pathway; once it is acquired, application practice can follow. It is important to be clear about the "wants" (through visualization, Chapter 10) and the priority of each outcome (aligned to values or critical paths) in order to achieve the desired outcome: the new and better you.

Consider values. An important personal value for me is authenticity. As a result, I prioritize activities that lead to more authentic relationships. The 4Rs and rapport become the first priority, given their alignment to my value system. Once I have the 4Rs and rapport, my filtering system seeks and sends authentic relationship opportunities to my conscious mind. My reticular activating system works to achieve the outcome; I see new opportunities, not previously visible, to practice the technique until it is effortless and comfortable. The system works because I am focusing on what matters, what is important, and what I want; the rest of the information is noise and will be "buried" away before I have the chance to realize that it was ever there.

This process repeats for each mini outcome or milestone until there is a clear path for the journey you are about to undertake. In practice, I find that individuals do well when the outcome and its associated mini outcomes (or milestones) are visualized in a collage, drawing, graphic, or video allowing regular and immediate recall of the big picture. This is a powerful way to reinforce the outcome and to refresh the reticular activating system filters as the plan is being executed.

YOUR TURN, GIVE IT A TRY!
Align your Disney Creative Strategy plan and your PECSAW plan with your future self to develop a powerful visual motivator for the generative outcome you seek. If you don't have these plans yet, choose an example from the book or make up your own for a relatively quick self-improvement activity.

Your toolbox is filling up with each progressive chapter, but we are not done yet! You've done some good self-reflection and established what you want and how to get there, and you're well on the way to executing the plan. Now is a good time to consider support systems. These need to be in place to help if you feel like you're reaching a plateau in your application of the desired skill, feel like giving up, or simply need a pep talk!

Chapter 13

Seeking Cheerleaders

When I say cheerleaders, of course I don't literally mean those in the NFL (or the equivalent). Cheerleaders in our context means resources you can call upon anytime to support you in your journey. There are two types:

1. Virtual resources
2. Physically present resources

VIRTUAL RESOURCES

These resources are effectively accessible to you 24 hours a day, 7 days a week, 365 days a year as you work through delivering on your plan. There are two particularly helpful techniques, the Panel of Experts and the Circle of Resources. The primary purpose of these techniques is to harness your positive, resourceful qualities and bring them into your consciousness as you need them. A question inevitably surfaces at this stage: "What should I experience when I apply either of these techniques?"

It's a great question. There are a few specific things that help create the environment and establish the conditions when you are first acquiring the techniques. I say "first" because once you have them in your toolbox, you can call on them anytime and anywhere.

- It starts with a comfortable space. Comfortable may be a quiet space surrounded by personal things or a more active space with ambient noise (for me, it is my study where I have a favorite chair, my own artwork, and some prized books).
- Visualizing can occur in several ways: Milestones or recent experiences are particularly powerful but it could also be one or more successful moments. For me, it tends to be the wedding day, the birth of a child, a career milestone (such as a promotion, starting at a new company, or winning an award), as I can remember these events in vivid detail, complete with all the emotion of the experience, as if it were yesterday. The key is selecting personally powerful experiences.
- Choosing a trigger is a breeze. Some common triggers include colors, shapes, objects (e.g., a favorite sweater or car), symbols (e.g., an emoji or yin and yang), or small physical movements (e.g., poking a finger into the palm's fleshy part, curling toes, or tapping a foot). My own trigger is a circular column, which is a by-product of being a Star Trek fan (and transporters).
- Next is approaching the technique with an open mind and trusting that it works as effortlessly as it sounds. Keeping an open mind is easy for you—you're reading this book to do just that!
- The final step is understanding the technique sequence and then using your chosen location, memory experiences, trigger, and mindset. Practice, practice, and practice again until it is quick and effortless for you.

These techniques are rapidly assimilated—it takes minutes, not days—after which you can call upon the resource qualities and experience the state you want (feel confident, feel energetic, or feel creative, for example) when you need it.

Skill mastery is an ideal opportunity to use both of these virtual resources.

Panel of Experts

Your Panel of Experts is most effective in assisting you to—

- Learn from prior experiences
- Visualize yourself in excellence

The basic technique involves recalling a specific time in which you were applying the skill you seek to master, and it just wasn't going as planned. Imagine that you are watching a movie of that specific moment. You see it all playing out in front of you. Rate your unfavorable feelings about this moment on a scale of 1 to 10, with 1 being lightly unfavorable and 10 being extremely unfavorable.

Now, it's time to switch gears and establish an imaginary expert panel. Your panel needs to be personalized; its composition is most effective when it includes the following:

1. A master in the skill you are seeking (someone *you* admire)
2. A wise individual (someone real or fictional who is wise in *your* eyes)
3. A humorist (someone *you* find funny)
4. You on your best day

Now replay the movie again, with you (in the film) adopting the mind-set (or attitude) of each of your panel members in turn. (Note: You're only adopting their attitude and style, *not* their behaviors in the movie.)

Select the ideal panelist persona for the situation (which might include one or possibly more than one individual), and imagine yourself performing the skill using the panelist persona's mindset. See how it feels to adopt this modified mindset (or style). Keep at it until you identify the right one for your needs, one that feels comfortable and produces the outcome you want.

Once you've made your choice, there are three additional steps to complete in order to imprint your new mindset and replace the old unfavorable or unproductive one.

Using your movie moment, adopt and associate with your new mindset in each step:

1. Replay the original moment but observe an ending that is as you originally imagined: on fire!
2. Use an upcoming situation that is similar in nature. Crystallize the association of the positive outcome with your new mindset in this scenario.
3. Use an upcoming situation that is dissimilar in nature but where this new mindset would be useful. Apply this new mindset and visualize the positive outcome once again.

This imprinting process will allow you to extend the mindset and approach to future scenarios where you want to do the desired skill, or to other unrelated situations where this new mindset or approach could be useful to you in achieving the outcome you seek.

Circle of Resources

The second technique, the Circle of Resources, is particularly helpful in breaking through a plateau. In NLP terms, it is commonly referred to as the Circle of Excellence or Ring of Power.

Your Circle of Resources is used to:

- Get into a positive state of mind
- Reframe unpleasant feelings
- Break and reset a negative frame of mind or thought process

The basic technique involves remembering a couple of strongly positive memories with which you will associate and anchor so you can later call upon this resourceful state when it will help you in a particular moment.

The process

1. Recall two or three strongly positive memories from your life. Choose those that are most vivid in their good feeling for you.
2. Choose a color (perhaps a favorite) and choose an object, sound, word, or some other mechanism. You want a subtle trigger. The trigger will help you discreetly call upon the resource later on when you need it. (Hint: Trigger discretion is important, as one day you may need to call upon the resource in a room full of people.)
3. Now imagine or visualize a shape (a circle, square, or something similar) in front of your feet, in your chosen color.
4. Within the shape you've chosen, visualize ("see") yourself experiencing one of your positive memories. Make a mental note of how you look, sound, and feel in that particular moment.
5. When your chosen memory is clear and strong, physically take a step into your chosen shape. Allow yourself to feel surrounded by the positive feelings and blanketed by your colored shape. Visualize your object (or hear your chosen sound or your chosen word) as your colored shape completely envelops you.
6. Stay in the moment, sensing everything good about it, until you start to hear your inner chatter about the chosen experience, then

physically step out of the shape to disassociate from it. (Inner chatter within your Circle of Resources is unhelpful; hence, step out to prevent that.)

7. Repeat steps 4 through 6 for each of your memories. Your objective is to build each one of them together until this resource is strongly embedded with your chosen trigger.

Embedding the new behavior

Once you've completed steps 1 through 7, check your trigger to make sure it works properly; it should immediately create a resourceful state of mind through association. A resourceful state, for example, might be a positive state of mind, seeing opportunity in challenge, or feeling hope in a crisis.

For example, you could practice with a work meeting that didn't quite go according to plan because one of the participants challenged your ideas in a personal way, leaving you with an unpleasant feeling about the experience. Or, use the technique to help you prepare for a public speaking engagement where you might be feeling anxious or need to "be on fire" throughout. The technique provides reassurance by creating relaxation to support you before you walk on stage (or during your delivery if your resource is more likely to be required then).

Place your new resource in your personal toolbox. Call upon it whenever it would be beneficial to you!

YOUR TURN, GIVE IT A TRY!

Create your personalized Panel of Experts and anchor your Circle of Resources. Practice until it is effortless to call up the resources.

PHYSICALLY PRESENT RESOURCES

In addition to virtual resources, living, human resources are invaluable in the right context. Some individuals refer to these resources as mentors, though the technique I have used and promoted throughout my career is broader than mentorship.

I call the concept a "personal board (of directors)." The goal is access to a diverse group of people with whom you can brainstorm ideas, discuss opinions, solicit feedback, or stress-test something. Your board is a useful resource throughout your life, where members will rotate on and off as your life changes. Ideally, consider developing a board predominantly outside of your working group, simply because it provides greater diversity, impartiality, and often confidentiality. The key criteria in selecting the best individuals for your board are as follows:

Value alignment: It is important to share personally critical values (such as integrity, honesty, open-mindedness, loyalty, etc.).

Committed to your success: This plays out in the quality of your discussions, depth of feedback, and time commitments.

Diversity of experience: This attribute helps you to avoid tunnel vision or surrounding yourself with "yes" people. You are seeking individuals willing to challenge you and help you grow.

Diversity of worldview: This attribute helps you understand broader cultural, personal, or language nuances in a given situation.

You can, of course, add other attributes that are important to you; however, these are the core ones found in a balanced "personal board." If you are wondering how to approach individuals to join your board, simply use the techniques covered in Chapter 4 (Preparing) and Chapter 5 (Conducting), just as you did in approaching experts.

Let's look at board benefits in action.

Example

Prisha has just been promoted to management, and she's full of ideas and motivated to make a positive contribution to the organization! Her team members are battle weary, as this is their fourth team supervisor in a year; they've been down this path many times. Prisha holds her first team meeting and runs into resistance with one particularly disruptive team member; the rest sit quietly waiting for Prisha to explode (it's been their typical experience). Prisha is at a loss for words. She listens and then ends the meeting with: "Let's all go away, think about this discussion, and reconvene in one week." She walks back to her desk, feeling deflated, wondering where it went off track and how to turn the situation around.

It is obvious to Prisha that she needs to call her personal board for help. What should she ask for and who might be the best placed to help her?

Values: This element is already embedded in the personal board she selected. The values that matter here are open-mindedness, integrity, and service to others.

Committed: As with values, this is embedded in her personal board. She will need their time, their willingness to guide her in finding a path forward, and their ability to be honest in the conversation (even if the message is a hard one).

Diversity of experience: This is where she gets selective. She will need a member with experience in leadership coaching or practical experience dealing with difficult conversations, forming teams (sometimes called forming, storming, norming, and performing[16]), and transitioning to management.

Diversity of worldview: This attribute is helpful when dealing with virtual teams (those that sit in multiple locations), where often culture, language, and demographic differ.

---

16   Bruce Tuckman, 1965, "Developmental Sequence in Small Groups."

This combination of skills and attributes in a board member are typically found in HR professionals, professional coaches, and senior management. Prisha can call on the board member with this combination for support before the next meeting, enabling her to be prepared for a one-to-one with the "disruptive" team member followed by the entire team.

She calls Diego. He's a chief people officer with over fifteen years of experience; he's seen most things! After a lengthy discussion, he gives Prisha this advice:

- Do a "getting to know you and each other" team exercise (focus on camaraderie before deliverables).
- Share what you stand for as a leader (your priorities, how you evaluate performance, how you want the team to work, and your open-door policy).
- Share the team goals (establishing ambitious but achievable goals).
- Execute quick wins (look for team member pain points and solve them swiftly, such as inefficient and outdated processes).

Prisha reflects on Diego's insights and suggestions. She holds a team meeting a week later. Using Diego's approach, she engages the team members—especially the disruptive one. That day, she earns capital and inspires with a new and clear direction. Mission accomplished (of course, she needs to continue to deliver on her promise).

Plateaus can be disrupted using one or all of these techniques to reframe your mindset, which in turn influences your behavior. Drawing on new or energized resources is effective in breaking free of being "stuck."

YOUR TURN, GIVE IT A TRY!

Use a current example in your work or personal life where you need a bit of a lift up to get "unstuck." Run the scenario using one (or several) of these techniques. Observe the impact to your mindset/ attitude. Practice it until it is effortlessly effective.

Chapter 14

Assessing Achievements

We've reached the brilliant point in the journey where you take stock of your progress. You are wondering if you're hitting the right high notes. What do your "customers" (anyone on the receiving end of you applying your chosen skill) think and feel after interacting with you doing your thing? Are they eager to do so again or dreading the next experience? How are you feeling about your own performance of the skill?

There are many questions you could ask yourself to assess your performance. One approach I found that works well is being "customer driven" in your assessment approach, that is, putting yourself in the shoes of your "customers." For example, as a pianist, is your audience moved by the music and transported away as you play? Good question! How could you objectively assess that (because after all, there is no point in kidding yourself if the objective is skill mastery)? I favor an inside-out assessment approach (Figure 14.1), which we look at next.

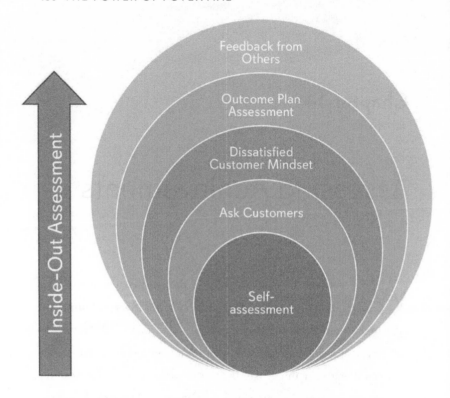

Figure 14.1. Inside-out achievement assessment model.

SELF-ASSESSMENT

The first step is to look at your own skill habits. The reason we look at ourselves first is the recognition that the outcome is directly influenced by our own competencies and behaviors. If we haven't embedded key skill elements yet, it is almost certainly going to lead to a sub-optimal outcome. Questions you can ask yourself are:

- Is the outcome plan (see Chapter 11) designed for maximum efficiency and effectiveness?
- Are the principles, techniques, tools, and insights that you have gained from your experts being consistently and regularly applied?
- Are they second nature yet? If not, what more could be done?

Having looked inward first and cleared that hurdle in assessing performance (meaning there are no significant deficiencies), we can move outward.

ASK CUSTOMERS

The obvious external first step is to identify what your "customers" want and expect in the first place, and determine whether they are getting value for their investment (investment here could be time or money or both). This knowledge sets the benchmark against which the quality of your skill is assessed. The best way to do this is simply to ask them. Get into the habit of regularly meeting in person or via video calls to set up this dialogue; go one step further and offer alternative ways to connect. Ask a handful of relevant questions where customers can tell you in their own words if/how you are meeting (and hopefully exceeding) expectations. Listen for what is said and what is not said; sometimes the latter is more insightful (use the techniques in Chapter 5). Post-activity surveys are a useful tool for feedback, anonymized or not. These work well in business settings to debrief on performance, in public speaking by asking the audience, or in social settings when asking friends and family how <insert the skill> was for them. Direct "customer" feedback is generally the most objective assessment mechanism available.

Indirect assessments augment the feedback. For example, assessing the frequency of referral is a helpful indicator of the positive impact your skill is having. Forward-looking anticipatory analysis—anticipating the needs of others for your particular skills, perhaps before they even realize they need your talent—is a way to future-proof your skills and perhaps the next best way to assess performance.

A good example of this is Apple and the introduction of the iPhone. Some (probably most, to be fair) customers wondered, "Why do I need all this technology in a phone?" Apple foresaw the need (or perhaps created the need) before the market did. Less than a decade later, smartphones are ubiquitous. What does Apple do well? They effectively anticipate user needs, listen, and improve upon the products. This is the ideal continuous outcome for skill improvement.

DISSATISFIED CUSTOMERS

A second effective external assessment is imagining yourself as a dissatisfied "customer." Write down all of the things that didn't go according to plan, leading to a sub-optimal experience. Let's use public speaking to illustrate this mindset:

- The sound was dreadful, the audio was cutting in and out, and in some parts of the room the speaker's microphone created screeching feedback.
- The speaker was dull and uninteresting and lacked passion, charisma, and confidence, leading to audience members leaving throughout the sixty-minute slot.
- The venue itself was too small; audience members were crammed in the aisles on plastic chairs.

With this list, target half or more of the issues you can positively impact immediately and fix them!

OUTCOME PLAN ASSESSMENT

Compare your process against the detailed outcome plan (Chapter 11) by assessing the following:

- What remaining mini outcomes need to be accomplished?
- When do they need to be completed by?
- What resources are needed to get them completed?
- What is the impact on the broader outcome if these mini outcomes are not done?
- Has the achievement assessment identified gaps in the original plan that need to be remedied?
- How is the TATE model (Chapter 4) meeting its objective in communicating your progress to you?

(Hint: Use the 4Rs with your self-assessment. You are not looking to rip yourself down. Rather, you are looking for opportunities to further improve. That is a positive way forward!)

Here, the goal is to self-assess your progress toward your plan, including a critical analysis of possible gaps or issues. What you identify in this step may cause your plan itself to be modified. This is normal when you first start applying the model to skill development. Once the techniques in the book are second nature, you can effortlessly repeat them for new skill development or mastery . . . just like learning to walk. Those first steps, all those years ago, took significant effort; now they are effortless.

FEEDBACK FROM OTHERS

Last, but by no means least, simply ask others around you for feedback on your progress. Are you asking your personal board, colleagues, friends, and family to share their experiences with you (like Prisha did)? How are you stress-testing your ideas about what "customers" need and expect with one or more of these circles? What feedback questions are you using—open or closed questions? Remember, closed questions lead to yes or no answers, whereas open questions lead to an explanation (Chapter 5).

There are numerous ways to assess achievements, progress, or outcomes, starting from inside oneself and swiftly moving outside. There is nothing worse than someone who thinks they are amazing when consensus shows the opposite. This happens especially to individuals in a position of power where either no feedback is solicited at all or the feedback received is summarily dismissed. Beware of these self-defeating traps. Feedback is critical, as we are all only ever as good as we are *perceived* to be!

YOUR TURN, GIVE IT A TRY!
Using a skill you are currently working to improve or perfect (could be a small skill or a significant one), capture the assessment results for two of the techniques above to determine how you are doing relative to both your own expectations and those of a trusted circle around you.

Hint: Remember to use the 4Rs and the feedback received to improve upon your plan or execution (as the case may be).

We are nearing the end of the implementation journey. Next, we cover reaching your outcome and what lies ahead after that. Let's get to work on that now.

Chapter 15

Reaching Your Destination

The ship is sailing toward the harbor, the destination is in sight—a rewarding feeling indeed after all the effort put in to get to this point! The normal question to be asking now is "How do I know if I am achieving at an expert level?" You certainly have a good basis from which to self-assess the answer, leveraging the input obtained from customers and others. However, is it enough? Do the stakeholders you asked know what expert looks and feels like? Have they experienced it themselves? Are their views aligned with reality or is the bar unrealistically "out there"? The criteria against which your expertise is evaluated are similar, whether you are assessing or being assessed. By knowing the typical attributes, you can also subjectively assess yourself throughout the journey.

WHAT ARE THE TYPICAL CRITERIA?

You are undoubtedly getting the picture: You need to tap into a specific demographic group in order to get feedback on whether you are perceived as an expert. Perception means that there will be no ironclad criteria; however, there are strong indicators to support the judgment:

1. Consistently successful performance: a track record of high and reliable performance of the skill in the past (recognizing that in reality some performance achievements come down to luck).

2. Depth and breadth of implied knowledge, such as the ability to identify patterns and relationships between things, the ability to see things others cannot (such as slight errors imperceptible to the average eye), the ability to anticipate outcomes, understanding complex concepts or systems, and making the complex simple (acknowledging that implicit knowledge is hard to articulate for many).

3. Peer recognition and respect: being seen by experts in the field as an expert yourself. Getting expert attention may be challenging; however, the power of social media can turn this around. A brilliant example of the use of experts to validate skill mastery is "Alex: French Guy Cooking," a popular YouTuber. His video diary of making the perfect omelet, as defined by Jacques Pepin, is both funny and educational. (Note: A caveat in peer recognition is possible cognitive bias with the halo[17] and horn[18] effects.)

4. Experience: the period over which the skill has been performed (typically measured in years). Generally, the longer the skill has been performed, the more perfected it is. Also consider the frequency of skill application, not just the number of years.

5. Self-reflective: Experts can pinpoint their last mistake in agonizing detail, typically because it eats away at them. Applying the 4Rs helps manage this tendency, hence its importance. (Some experts won't openly admit a mistake, and some individuals purporting to be experts say they've never made any.)

---

17 Frederick L. Wells, 1907. The halo effect occurs when we judge someone or something as entirely positive based on a single, favorable aspect. It can easily result in biased decisions.

18 E.L. Thorndike, 1920. The horn effect is the same cognitive bias principle found with the halo effect, except it attributes negative qualities to someone or something. It too can result in biased decisions.

6. Credentials: Experts commonly hold professional certifications or licensing. (However, degrees, certifications, or similar credentials only indicate a minimal competence level, not the achievement of expertise.)

Let's look at an assessment for a furniture designer and maker, where expertise is achieved.

Example

1. Consistently successful performance: winning industry design awards, high levels of repeat customers, and furniture pieces received by customers are in showroom condition.
2. Depth and breadth of knowledge: can take a customer's rough idea and bring it to life in ways that exceed the customer's expectations. Can suggest creative material alternatives (such as woods, finishes, or accessories) that the customer hasn't considered, sees imperfections in the piece and addresses it in production so it leaves the factory in pristine condition, and chooses materials based on their feel and aesthetic potential for a given piece.
3. Peer recognition: industry awards and cited by peers as an excellent example of technique, design, or quality.
4. Experience: practicing furniture design and making for over fifteen years, developing unique manufacturing techniques (such as a new joinery method or a new leg design).
5. Self-reflection: keenly aware of even the slightest imperfection, learns from it and adapts techniques or design accordingly. A feedback loop is embedded naturally within the end-to-end process.
6. Credentials: learned under a recognized master cabinetmaker, design accreditations, and now teaching a new generation of furniture designers and maker apprentices.

A furniture designer and maker who was not deemed an expert may simply meet a couple of the criteria but not most, or may achieve most of them but on an inconsistent basis, or may fail to achieve even one of the criteria.

WHO CAN OBJECTIVELY ASSESS YOUR SKILL?

With criteria in hand, which stakeholder demographic should we be approaching for this assessment (especially in the early days, as once you reach expertise, feedback needs change)? The best and most readily accessible sources are the experts identified in Chapter 3. Typically, the time they invested with you already results in a desire to see you succeed which tends to facilitate obtaining feedback at this point.

Remember to practice all of the communication techniques covered in Part One (in particular, Chapter 5); you want the exchange to be rich and open. Once you've obtained feedback, be sure to incorporate it as self-improvement mini outcomes within the wider outcome plan. Ignoring constructive feedback often results in a loss of the expert's goodwill with his or her time. This occurs when an individual feels they've taken the time to give you something and you've ignored it (that is, there is no feedback loop at all), and this perception can directly influence subsequent behavior.

In the end, there is significant leverage or latitude in making an expertise assessment. The key point to take away is that it is normal to continuously strive for better—but too much perfection and rigidity kills off creativity and passion! Find a good and sustainable balance for your desired outcome. Expertise will follow before you realize it.

Chapter 16

Don't Stop Now . . .

Let's recap where we are in the skill mastery process. So far, you've—

1. Developed a final model of the skill you want to perfect, after a ton of work with experts
2. Gained a clearer understanding of what drives you (motivation)
3. Learned how to use your change strengths and manage blind spots advantageously
4. Dreamt of mastering a skill, framed it positively, and stress-tested it
5. Converted the dream into a plan with tangible outcomes, priorities, and critical dependencies
6. Started actively executing on your plan to perfect the desired skill
7. Surrounded yourself with a support system fit for the journey
8. Started assessing your performance, subjectively (you) and objectively (others)
9. Course-corrected the plan to reflect feedback insights and takeaways
10. Defined how to recognize when expertise is achieved

Take a moment to appreciate the magnitude of your accomplishmen (Figure 16.1) so far . . . this is no small feat!

Figure 16.1. Your toolbox of skills from our journey.

Okay, let's move into the homestretch. You reach mastery, so wha and now what? That may sound flippant, but it isn't meant to be. It is jolting call to action: The time has come to become a teacher, a mento for peers, your team, colleagues, executives (it gets lonely at the top, too) friends, family, and children. The model can be applied (and adapted) fo any demographic.

How do you take these lessons and become a change champio to support others in their skill-development journey? We shoul start by understanding what change champions actually are. They ar individuals who—

- Understand and acknowledge the need and reasons for change as well as the ecosystem impacts that will result
- Set clear outcomes that are accomplished via the planned changes
- Understand and plan for "things" that may work for or against their journey

Change champions remove barriers to change while simultaneously creating support for the change.[19] This is initially accomplished effectively using the Disney Creative Strategy and then stress-testing or checking the dream (change) against an individual's ecosystem via the Enhanced Personality Map (Chapter 5). The next step is understanding what is needed, why it is needed, and why it matters (via expert interviews). The culmination of these interviews is the development of a final detailed model of the skill (Chapter 8).

As teachers and change champions, we only light the way once the decision to change something is made by the individual themselves. In other words, we are facilitators, not authoritarians.

Beyond change champion, there is of course an additional role that you can play: teacher. You've decided you want to continue this journey. You're excited about the chance to use your newly developed skill replication model to create a market-ready product or service. Or possibly you're considering teaching others a specific skill, the modeling project for the skill itself. This outcome is one that I cover extensively in my next book[20], on launching your modeling business idea.

Imagine a world in which poverty, hunger, power, and greed don't exist—what could we accomplish if every human being truly had equal

---

19 Porter Lynch, 2012.

20 Expected to be published in 2022

opportunity and the freedom to explore? Inspire others by sharing what you've accomplished here, leading by doing, and applying your new mindset, attitude, and behaviors. Show everyone that anything is possible once you know the secret. The possibilities are infinite and you can make a difference now! And, perhaps most crucially, have fun doing it!

You're All Set!

Our journey has taken us from a big idea through self-improvement and perfection of a desired skill. What might have started as a mere personal interest has elegantly evolved. A new mastered skill beckons to be used! Whether you decide to use the tips, tricks, and tools shared in this book to improve yourself or to help others do the same is a personal choice. What really matters is that you embark on a meaningful path for yourself, with no regrets.

We covered two phases together. In Part One we unlocked the model's secrets, looking specifically at how to

1. Generate ideas
2. Refine your chosen idea
3. Develop a prototype model of the skill/idea
4. Confirm that the model works
5. Finalize it and share it

In Part Two we explored how to take the model created from the experts' worlds into your own skills toolbox, specifically how to

1. Clarify your endgame
2. Establish a winning game plan
3. Get it done already!
4. Surround yourself with the best support system
5. Enjoy the fruit of your labor

You now possess the secret to learning and perfecting new skills. Regret is a thing of the past. You have the potential, the tools, the power, and the confidence to take on something new, something fun, to further a career, to make more money—or simply to do something you love better.

The Appendix contains additional reference material to support your journey. I have included a useful cheat sheet of the key insights for you to pin somewhere visible as a gentle reminder.

You might also wish to explore further the fascinating and powerful world of Neuro-linguistic Programming and communication; it is an experience that doesn't disappoint.

The world is your oyster. Make it a better place to be, and help others do the same!

Acknowledgments

The inspiration for this book occurred in Purbeck, England, thanks to the encouragement of an inspiring team of NLP instructors and master practitioners, and to a certain comedic modeling project presentation. (You each know who you are!)

I want to thank each and every one of you for being part of that enriching journey.

To all the experts who have graciously shared their knowledge, insights, experiences, and opinions with me, most grateful thanks. In particular, Lynda Hawton Kitamura, Lizzi Larbalestier, Wendy McLeod, Gurbeen Bhasin, Derek Sidebottom, Reg Connolly, and Colin Reay—you inspired me to build on what we shared together with those who want to invest in their most important asset: themselves.

To the editing team who helped me tell this compelling story, you were the mechanical engineers that worked on my moon-shot rocket! In particular, Alice McVeigh and Carolyn Roark for your endless patience and support—you are stars.

To the illustrator at *Scribes Like Us* who helped me create a character that blends my likeness and a certain fictitious spy, Waples . . . Charles Waples, thank you for humoring me!

To all of the team at Greenleaf Book Group, I valued the wise counsel and support throughout the publishing process. In particular, Jen Glynn for keeping everyone on track during the production schedule—cat herders have nothing on Jen!

Appendix

Additional Reference Material

Circle of Resources, David Wray © 2021,
https://davidwray.com/index.php/circle-of-resources/

Goal Setting, David Wray © 2021,
https://davidwray.com/index.php/goal-setting-pecsaw/

Panel of Experts, David Wray © 2021,
https://davidwray.com/index.php/panel-of-experts/

First Two Minutes of Public Speaking, David Wray © 2021,
https://davidwray.com/index.php/overcoming-a-fear-of-public-speaking/

Change Your Thinking Pattern—Anchors, David Wray © 2021,
https://davidwray.com/index.php/knowledge-base-2/change-your
-thinking-pattern-anchors/

Public Speaking—A Common Fear Easily Overcome,
FCGS © 2013–2021, frameworkcoaching.com/public-speaking-a
-common-fear-easily-overcome/

Desired Skill Outcome Template (Fishbone Style & Editable),
David Wray © 2021, https://davidwray.com/index.php/desired-skill
-outcome-template-fishbone-style/

Answer Key for "Your Turn Challenges"

CHAPTER 4: PREPARE TO INTERVIEW

Depth of Knowledge answer guide:

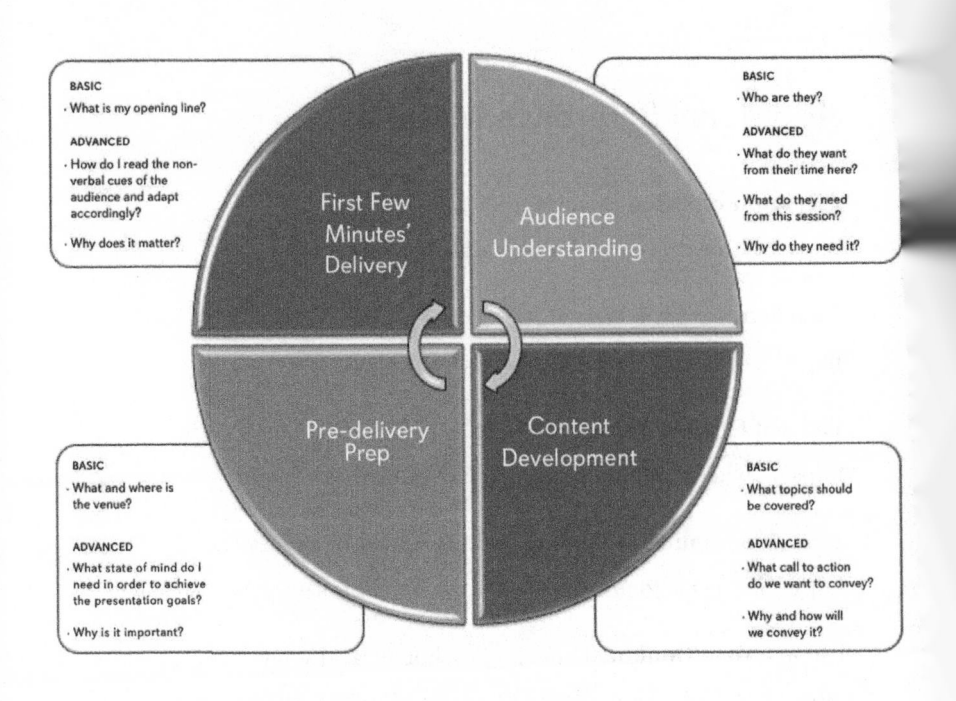

First Few Minutes' Delivery

BASIC
- What is my opening line?

ADVANCED
- How do I read the non-verbal cues of the audience and adapt accordingly?
- Why does it matter?

Audience Understanding

BASIC
- Who are they?

ADVANCED
- What do they want from their time here?
- What do they need from this session?
- Why do they need it?

Pre-delivery Prep

BASIC
- What and where is the venue?

ADVANCED
- What state of mind do I need in order to achieve the presentation goals?
- Why is it important?

Content Development

BASIC
- What topics should be covered?

ADVANCED
- What call to action do we want to convey?
- Why and how will we convey it?

Your Personal Toolbox

Here is a visual summary of all of the tools and techniques covered in the book to support your lifelong success.

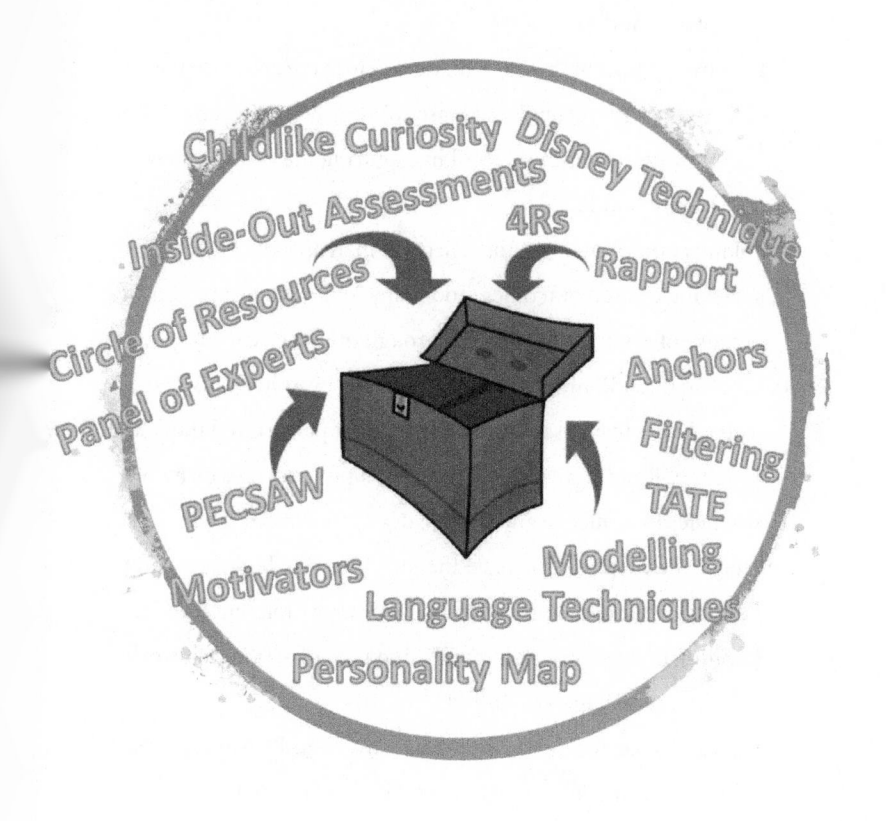

Useful Cheat Sheet Process Reminders

1. Identify specific areas of interest when selecting your experts (Chapters 1 and 3).

2. In conversations with your experts, attempt to capture details objectively, without applying biases of your own. Keeping a clear, "unknowing" mindset is useful in capturing the expert's view (Chapters 4 and 5).

3. Taking appropriate time for reflection increases the likelihood of achieving desired outcomes. Too many "good intentions" misfire because of skipping or rushing through this step (Chapter 6).

4. Validate the skill model you've developed, by either expert walk-through or a live observation of the expert performing their skill in action. Resolve missing or redundant process steps or inconsistencies in sequence and use the description from the first draft model you prepared to create the final model (Chapters 7 and 8).

5. Leverage your own motivational and change preference understanding to develop a skill-acquisition plan of action that works best for you (Chapters 9 and 11).

6. Prioritize your time and eliminate distractions by using a crystal-clear picture of the outcome you seek (Chapter 12).

7. Surround yourself with a support system that guides you to success with help and feedback how, where, and when you need it (Chapters 13 and 14).

8. Use your newfound skills to lift others into a space of new and previously unimaginable possibilities, and have fun doing so (Chapter 16).

Glossary

Term	Definition
Commonalities	Within any one of the six building blocks of the Personality Map, an attribute consistently found among all experts and experts-in-training
Differences	The strategy that an expert uses to perform a particular behavior or complete a particular activity that is not yet found in aspiring experts-in-training
DMD	Differences that make a difference
KM	Knowledge Management
Micro-moments	The small steps or actions that when done together result in the skill
Personality Map	A tool for organizing thoughts, information, and communication as well as understanding what makes a person behave as they do
TATE	Trigger, Action, Target, Exit
TOTE	Test, Operate, Test, Exit

About the Author

For over twenty years, David has been a passionate transformation and change management executive. He has worked with Fortune 100 companies and individuals throughout the Americas, Europe, the Middle East, and Asia.

Seeing firsthand how many people struggle—and often give up—while trying to learn new skills, he wondered why some manage it almost effortlessly. During this quest to understand the "differences that make a difference", he discovered their secrets.

In his new book, *The Power of Potential: A Straightforward Method for Mastering Skills from Personal to Professional*, David shares these secrets to illustrate how they apply in business and everyday life—sharing many practical tips, tricks, and tools that have helped many others achieve their personal and professional goals.

When David is not leading, mentoring or coaching, he can be found diving somewhere spectacular in our beautiful blue planet with his wife, Martha.

Made in the USA
Las Vegas, NV
20 February 2021